Baboons, Oceans, and a Cookie Jar

A Grief Journey

BRYAN A. ANDERSON

STORYLINE
PRESS

Storyline Press
ISBN: 978-0-578-34192-7 (paperback)
Baboons, Oceans, and a Cookie Jar: A Grief Journey
Copyright © 2023 Bryan Anderson

Cover Design by: Diana Lawrence
Interior Design by: Lisa Parnell

Unless otherwise noted, all Scripture quotations are from Holy Bible, New International Version®, NIV®, Copyright © 2011 by Biblica, Inc.® Used by permission. All rights reserved worldwide.
    Scripture quotations marked ESV are from the ESV® Bible (The Holy Bible, English Standard Version®), copyright © 2001 by Crossway, a publishing ministry of Good News Publishers. Used by permission. All rights reserved.
    Scripture quotations marked NASB 1995 are from the NASB 1995® Bible (The Holy Bible, New American Standard Version 1995®), copyright © 1995 by Lockman Foundation. Used by permission. All rights reserved.

Manufactured in the United States of America

10 9 8 7 6 5 4 3 2 1

Dedication

To My Baboon, who lives in the tall grass,

Jesus has you now. Soon He will have me.
I can't wait to see you again, my beautiful daughter.

Love,
Dad

Contents

Contents

Contents

Introduction

My youngest daughter died Thanksgiving morning 2021 at the age of nineteen. Her death was accidental. During the months that followed, I sought out help to guide me through a grief I could not comprehend and healing that seemed an impossibility when I started out. The book you now hold in your hand came from my own journey and was necessary for my own healing.

I had two goals for writing this book. First, I needed to preserve her memory! The fear of forgetting her life drove me to the completion of this book while the memories and experiences were still fresh and had not faded with the passage of time. Second, I needed to process her death with God. I learned only God had the capacity to heal my wounds in a way that brought closure—removing the sting, fear, and darkness that had invaded my life in every facet where my daughter had touched my life. The book you now hold is a compilation of thirty-seven stories and a letter to my daughter, most of them written within the first year after her death.

It is deeply personal. It is raw in emotion. My heart was the quill pen, my tears the ink that created this book. There are things and moments I hesitate to share yet it was part of my healing, so they are included. It is what it is. I shared some of these stories with others who were grieving their own loss, and many found them helpful on their own paths toward healing and wholeness. So, I am sharing these stories with you in the hope you can find them helpful in your own unwanted journey of loss.

I have scattered many lighthearted moments of Beatrice's life throughout the book, such as story 8: "Bats, Mushrooms, and Split Pea Soup" and story 16: "Woolly Buffalo." These and many other stories capture much of Beatrice's life and spirit through my eyes.

The first four stories, however, are intense and painful yet filled with unimaginable hope. They capture the day I heard the news and the immediate days afterward. They should be read together as one continuous event and with one underlying emotion—a father's heart crushed beyond the reach and comfort of human hands, trying his best to hold up a grieving family and navigate those days. If it was not for the intervention of God in the midst of those early days, I would have not had the courage nor, reluctantly I must admit, the will and desire to participate in this life anymore. I say this in hindsight as I reflect on the immeasurable struggles of this past year. Life hurts! How God worked with me during those early days laid the foundation on which I was able to mourn and cling to Him for healing through the many dark days that followed that Thanksgiving morning. My stories highlight His role in providing light to a soul that dwelt in shadows and healing to a fractured heart.

My Beloved Beatrice

The thirty-seven stories and concluding letter will provide a richer and deeper description and appreciation of what made Beatrice, Beatrice. I tried to capture every important memory God brought to my mind. For now, I will share this about her:

Beatrice was a tender, joyful, and whimsical spirit with an impish grin. She saw life in a beautiful and playful way and was full of surprises. She also possessed a sharp and keen mind. She was an absolute delight to raise, and I loved being her father. Beatrice was a wonderful and loyal friend to many and cultivated those relationships and made them a priority. She left behind a legacy and spirit of friendship that was truly remarkable and one to be emulated by all. She loved much and was loved. She is deeply missed!

An Unwanted Path toward Healing

Healing from any loss, especially the death of a loved one, does not come easily nor quickly. It is a bitter shadow that follows and inflicts deep hurt. God's comfort can seem distant. Darkness becomes one's only dance partner. Unanswered questions chain the way forward. What if this loss has no meaning nor purpose? Is all of this just shrouded in absurdity, waste, and cruelty? How can God make something beautiful, redemptive, restorative, and whole from this death?

I found it took courage to go into this dark abyss of loss stemming from death and wait for God to respond. It was in my vulnerability He started to heal my wound and brought life and a new purpose to my remaining days. I do have a permanent scar now. I will always carry it with me. However, I also have a life God has invited me to live and one I am excited to live. Thus, scar and life will venture forth together, sorrow's hand holding onto joy's hand.

It is my prayer this book will help you in your journey of sorrow and grief and enable you to experience the richness of life once again. More importantly, I hope you will discover God has not abandoned you and instead is at hand, eager and able to heal you and renew your days when all you can see now is winter shadows and death.

The First Days:
AN UNWANTED CALL

Thanksgiving
Christ Will Return and Restore All

November 2021

"She's dead!" The hysterical scream on the other end of the phone was my oldest daughter. Anguish and disbelief filled the air as she sobbed. Folks nearby turned to see what was going on, as I screamed, "No, no, no, no . . . !" These were my first words. This cannot be happening. This was not supposed to happen. This was not her fate. Beatrice was dead. An eternity of thoughts wrapped up in a paused and monstrous moment of time. "No, no, no, no . . . !"

I was out for a walk and sitting on a bench on my church's property that Thanksgiving morning. This was a place I had often visited to reflect and meditate on God and my life with Him. This was the place I was sitting when the call came. I spoke to my daughter and tried my best to comfort her. I needed to put my own grief on hold to support her and reassure her everything would be OK. We would get through this together. "Lord???" I prayed!

All the flights leaving my small town were done for Thanksgiving, so I had to wait until Friday to begin the trip to New Jersey from Oregon. Family and friends took care of me. Somehow, I was able to pack what I would need for my time on the East Coast. Everything was a blur. Numbness had set in. I did not sleep much that night. My thoughts were an unwelcome companion during that first empty night. The alarm clock was set hours before the sun would rise on a day where the swirling gray of a nor'easter would have mirrored my soul. I think it was sunny.

Snacks and lunch had been packed for me, though food was more of an instrument to stir my wondering mind, lost in grief. I either slept or prayed the duration of the flight. I recalled all the stories where either Jesus or one of the prophets had given dead children back to their parents alive and prayed each story back to my heavenly Father, hoping for a miracle. What else was a father supposed to do? I had eight hours of flight time ahead of me, and so until He says otherwise, I felt no need to accept something He has the power to undo. However, I also knew I needed a final answer to my prayer by the time we landed. I needed the Holy Spirit's help, if the answer was no, to support my grieving oldest daughter. As the wheels touched the ground, the Lord spoke to my heart, "the trumpets will sound, the dead will rise, and those in Christ Jesus will rise first," referring to 1 Thessalonians 4:16. She was home with the Lord and was not coming back.

Jesus will return. I had not given deep thought to the return of Christ until that day. There is a day on the calendar when trumpets will be heard by all people, past and present. My daughter will experience a bodily resurrection. She will be given an imperishable body, where death will never be experienced again. Her faith in the atoning work of Christ for her sins on a blood-soaked cross and His bodily resurrection had ensured this future hope. This was now confirmed to me on an airstrip, west of the Hudson River, with a view of the New York City skyline.

A Cookie Jar
Thumbs up from Heaven

November 2021

M y prayer each morning was, "Holy Spirit, show me what to say, what not to say, and what to do." I prayed this prayer throughout the day. Like a close friend who knows how to take charge when your life has collapsed all around you, so was God during those first days in Jersey. This included helping me work with the funeral house to organize the memorial service for Beatrice. I coordinated with the funeral director and decisions were made collectively as a family; myself, oldest daughter and former wife.

We chose to cremate her body instead of having a burial. I also wanted to see her one last time. So I made arrangements with the funeral house to come in on Monday. Because we elected cremation, we also needed to purchase an urn for Beatrice's ashes, which I dropped off at the funeral house the day I saw my daughter for the last time on this earth. It is really not right that a parent experiences both the birth and death of their child, to witness the greatest of earthly joys and the deepest of life's sorrows in one brief lifetime.

We went as a family to a local antique shop to look for something that fit my daughter's personality. Something quirky. Perhaps a tea pot with a unique design. I prayed for God's guidance throughout the search. It was also a relief to all of us to get out of the house and do something as a family. It contributed to our remembrance and honoring of Beatrice instead of sitting and staring out the window, crying, unable to undo what had happened a few days ago.

After wandering through the shop for a while, we spotted a shelf with a large pitcher. It was nice but not quite right. As my eyes gazed at the other objects on the shelf, I spotted a 1970s vintage cookie jar that looked like a tree stump with mushrooms "growing" out of the lid. That was the urn.

I showed it to the rest of the family, and everyone agreed. I picked it up gently and held it tightly as if it were the most precious object in the entire world—and it was. We were grateful to find an urn for Beatrice, and this moment was filled with deep meaning and emotion as we found the perfect one, which captured her life through our eyes.

As we headed to the front of the shop to pay, I saw a vision of my daughter. Her face was beaming with approval and with two thumbs up. I could faintly hear her voice, "Way to go, Dad." I also knew Jesus was right next to her. I didn't see Him, but He was right next to my little sunshine. I smiled and soaked in the moment, basking in the joy of my daughter, knowing she was so joyful and knowing she was with my Jesus. How quickly you want to wrap up your life on this earth and be with Him and the one you loved who went before you.

The very next moment I said to the Lord and mainly to myself, "Lord, am I just imagining all of this?" It was a precious moment, but surely my own desires were wanting this vision to occur. Immediately, a scripture came flooding into my mind. It was the verse that had sustained my mother during the eighteen months my brother had battled with a glioblastoma tumor before he died some twelve years earlier. From the prophet Jeremiah, "Behold, I am the LORD, the God of all flesh. Is anything too hard for me?" (Jer. 32:27, ESV). I smiled and thanked the Lord for a beautiful gift of seeing my smiling daughter, thumbs up, and hearing her, "Way to go, Dad." I did good in her eyes!

Heaven is glorious. To be honest, I want my daughter back. I miss her. However, the look on her face said it all. "Dad, you have got to see this place." Though I might linger many years in the shadows of this world, the light and glory that is to come speaks of a grand place my heart longs to go. To see what my child sees, where my heart no longer hurts, and no crushing loss will ever be felt again but only joy.

The Funeral House

You Will Not Find the Living among the Dead

November 2021

I stood at the entrance of the room where they had my Beatrice laid. Time seems to lose its sense of importance when your world has collapsed around you. You stare blank-eyed, unable to grasp what has just occurred. Perhaps all this was a mistake; she cannot be dead! I had brought a dear friend with me for company. He waited in the next room to give me time alone. The urn was already safely in the hands of the funeral house director. It was now time.

Every part of me did not want to take the next step and see what I did not want to see. I broke down crying as I took the first step into the room. Those were the hardest steps I think a parent can take, to go and see your child for the last time on this earth. Seeing the coffin, seeing her, the hopeless thought formed in my head, *My dead child!* Yet as that thought was forming, the voice of the Holy Spirit thundered, "You will not find the living among the dead." These were the very words the angels had spoken to the women who were at the empty tomb, "Why do you look for the living among the dead?" (Luke 24:5). The words were being shouted at me, not in a way someone could overhear, but in God's normal way of communicating to our hearts and minds when we are fellowshipping with Him in prayer and in His Word.

As I walked toward the coffin, I was met with the same verse, over and over again, preempting my thought, "*my dead child,*" until I finally reached the place where my daughter's body lay. As I stood in front of the coffin, I finally accepted my Lord's view of the matter. She was not here in this body. To be honest, I am not sure if the Holy Spirit allowed me to hear those words in the voice of my Lord, my daughter's, or a combination of the two. Regardless, my heavenly Father made this truth crystal clear to me: my daughter was very much alive and with Him in His presence in heaven.

Death is not victorious. Death has lost its permanent sting. (See 1 Cor. 15:54–57.) I learned that without doubt on this day. The Lord was there, in an unexpected way, showing me His tenderness during the hardest time of my life. The hopelessness of an eternity without my daughter will never happen. Our separation is merely temporary, and for this I am grateful.

The Funeral House Continued
Go in Peace

November 2021

"Now what do I do with my time?" Once I had accepted that my Beatrice was very much alive in the presence of Jesus, the question emerged regarding what I should do next. I figured I would pray and thank God for my daughter's life and for the opportunity to enjoy it for these past nineteen years. After I prayed for a while, I was again at a loss about what to do next.

I had asked for a large chunk of time to be with her, and now less than ten minutes had passed. I turned around and sat facing away from her and decided to get my friend and see if he would be comfortable spending some time with my daughter and me. Our families had known each other for more than a decade and had attended the same church. What happened next was an unexpected gift from a loving Father to His grieving child. The Lord prompted us to hold a memorial service, right then, to celebrate the life of Beatrice.

There was going to be a bigger service a few days later, but the Lord had something uniquely planned for me this day. I gave a short tribute to Beatrice's life. My friend read Psalm 121. I had prayed this psalm over Beatrice's life for many years. We then sat down and cried as we listened to the lyrics of the song, *Scars in Heaven* by Casting Crowns, on my phone. It is a beautiful song about the hope of heaven—Christ in the midst of grieving the death of a loved one.

We got up from our chairs and worshipped the Lord. My friend then closed us in an amazing prayer. As he got toward the end of his prayer, the Lord spoke two things to me: "Well done" followed by "Go in peace," twice. I understood immediately. There was no need to dwell on the what-ifs and no need to have any regrets. All was good in heaven and thus was good on earth! Tears of joy and tears of sorrow!

No regrets. No what-ifs. I knew intuitively that focusing on those two things would not change the reality of the situation and would never bring my precious child back to life. I also knew they would haunt me and taunt me day and night, eating away my soul, if I allowed them. So, I knew how important those words from my Lord would be to me in the years to come. He knows me and knew I would focus on the unchangeable past, and He again preempted me with "Go in peace"—not once but twice—so I would know with absolute assurance! He loves too much to have it any other way.

An Unwanted Journey:
DARKNESS TO HEALING

It's a Girl
The Bringer of Joy

March 2002

Between Good Friday and Easter 2002, our Lord blessed us with the cutest bundle of happiness since our first daughter came into this world. We named her Beatrice, which means "Bringer of Joy." We selected her name because of the sorrow we endured trying to have our second child. My wife and I had suffered through two miscarriages prior to the birth of Beatrice. We were on edge the entire pregnancy until our precious child was born to us during the first weeks of spring.

Seeing her come into this world and hearing her first cries, we knew our prayers were answered. We were so grateful. Easter would be even more special and significant that year. A risen Lord and a new child who one day would desire Him and His cross. Also, her big sister would finally be able to see what was in mommy's tummy. I remember my oldest trying to hold Beatrice for the first time, with our help of course. It was such a cute photo.

We had selected Paige as her middle name. However, right before we were to sign the birth certificate, the Holy Spirit stopped us. Paige was not to be Beatrice's middle name. It was to be Ann, meaning "princess" or "grace." The Lord had named her Beatrice Ann Anderson. That is what He wanted.

She was a joy. A joy to us and to every life she touched. It comforts me to know He was actively involved in her birth. It reminds me to reflect on the many ways He was involved throughout her life for the nineteen years He blessed us with her presence, including the day He welcomed her into her eternal home with Him. My mind is drawn to David's psalm of his Shepherd and Beatrice's, "Surely goodness and mercy shall follow me all the days of my life, and I shall dwell in the house of the LORD forever" (Ps. 23:6, ESV). That is where Beatrice lives, in the house of the Good Shepherd (see John 10:11). Bea, when my days of walking on this earth are done, my little joy, would you do me the good pleasure of giving me the guided tour of the house of our Lord? I am sure He will join us, after all He was with us along every pasture, stream, path, and darkest valley while "dwell*[ed]*in the land of the shadow of death" (Isa. 9:2, KJV). I am sure it will be the best home tour I have ever seen!

The Accident
The Alpha and Omega

September 2002

"Beatrice, possible cracked head, heading to hospital, come home immediately." Those words, from the frantic voice on the other end of the phone, were spoken by my wife. She had tripped while holding our daughter, fell, and in the process slammed Beatrice's head onto the cement. My wife thought our daughter was dead on impact. Our baby cried and was still alive.

I informed my boss I had to leave immediately and got on a train from Penn Station, New York City, and headed west to our home in New Jersey. My wife was at the hospital when I arrived home. Our oldest daughter was with a neighbor. As I looked for the car key, a scripture came to mind, "the prayers of many" (2 Cor. 1:11). The apostle Paul was helped during a desperate time by the prayers of many believers, so I immediately phoned many of my dear friends and family to pray for Beatrice's life.

Before I left for the hospital, the Lord spoke one more scripture, "I am the Alpha and the Omega" (Rev. 1:8, ESV). He had Beatrice from the beginning of her life, her end, and all the in-betweens. I did not know whether she would live or die, but I knew He had every point of time covered. I left for the hospital with a deep peace, knowing that whatever happened, whether joy or sorrow, He was in charge of the final outcome. He was in charge of her life.

I arrived at the emergency area and quickly found my wife. Beatrice had gone through a CAT scan, and we were waiting for the doctor to review the results before speaking with us. My wife would be spending the night at the hospital with our daughter, so she headed home, during this pause, to retrieve some things. While she was gone, the doctor came out earlier than expected and discussed the findings with me. Beatrice had a cracked skull, and the next 24 hours were critical. Surgery might be needed in case fluids were developing in her brain. One of the miracles that day was having me hear the prognosis. When my wife returned later and asked me what the doctor had said, I couldn't remember the technical term he used, which would have caused my wife extreme stress. When the doctor returned the following day, the worst-case scenario was no longer on the table. God knew who best to tell the news.

Beatrice was kept in intensive care for six days, and then we brought her home. We needed to monitor her closely for the next six months as her head healed. Until then, I stayed fervent in my prayers. The day finally arrived, and the doctor cleared her. Beatrice's head had completely healed. The intense burden on my heart gave way to overwhelming gratitude to the God who answers, "the prayers of many."

The Alpha and the Omega. The beginning and the end. The first and last letters in the original language of the New Testament. I have no idea how many years I will be given. I had no idea Beatrice's life would be so short. Beatrice's life sits within the Alpha and Omega, bookends to the life He gave to her. I had His absolute assurance back then. I had to rediscover that truth again nineteen years later. It took me some time.

Walt Disney World Railroad
Put Away the Map

March 2005

Orlando, Florida! Home of Disney World, Sea World, Universal, and Flippers Pizzeria. We took our oldest child out of school, and the four of us headed south for seven days of warm weather and amusement parks. Escaping the long, cold East Coast winter was also a plus. We splurged for three nights at Disney's Animal Kingdom Lodge. The other four nights were at more moderate-priced accommodation. We also purchased the four-day Disney hopper pass, so we could enjoy dinner at EPCOT each night as we explored all four of Disney's amusement parks. We enjoyed different foods, and eating a different country's cuisine was one of the highlights of the trip!

Magic Kingdom was voted to be our first Disney Park to explore. The night before, I reviewed the map of the park and worked out our plan of attack to ensure we enjoyed most of the rides. Additionally, it was agreed we would arrive one hour before the park opened because we were allowed to enter early. The day would be perfect!

We arrived an hour after the park had opened! No worries, I had my map in my hand, and we would head immediately to the Jungle Cruise and then to the Pirates of the Caribbean and all would be good. Before starting our adventure, we needed to rent a stroller for Beatrice. She was turning four later that month, and her little legs would get very tired by the time the day was done. As we were grabbing the stroller, Beatrice noticed the Walt Disney World Railroad. She wanted us to ride it.

That's not part of the plan! More time lost! No worries, we can get on track once we get off "the slowest ride in the world"! Then we get off at the farthest possible point from the Jungle Cruise. Eyes buried in the map, agitation in my face, and encouraging everyone to head to our destination, I wanted to be in Adventure Land on the cruise. Instead, we boarded the railroad and headed to Fantasy Land, the exact opposite of where I wanted to be. My wife had seen enough! The only thing missing from the scene was a stepladder, so she could be eye to eye with me. I still remember every word on her tongue. "Put away the map before you ruin the whole trip," she said, glaring up with one of the most frightening looks and a voice to match. So, I did, and we all had an incredible time. That day I learned that sometimes maps and plans are best stuck in a pocket. Allow yourself the freedom to explore and experience life as God unfolds something infinitely better than a mapped-out plan. His ways are unmatched.

Plans change. All my plans ceased with Beatrice's death. I had no interest in formulating any plans that did not take her life into account. The script of her life did not end the way I had hoped, and now the script of my life had been engulfed in flames—only a pile of ashes remained. My attempts to create continuity, stability, and familiarity during the first year were frustrating. My grief had cast me into an ocean of pointlessness, and I was grasping for the nearest floating objects to help with this unwanted experience. Some were God's good plans for me, and some were not. All were grabbed with the intention of healing. All were ultimately taken away by God. The screams of grief for immediate and lasting comfort obscured the truth that the things of this earth would never heal my wounds. I had to quiet my screams and fears, put away my map of how life should unfold and what

I needed, and cling to Him. Listen to Him, regardless of the outcome. I am reminded of God's heart for His people: "For I know the plans I have for you," declares the LORD, "Plans to prosper you and not to harm you, plans to give you hope and a future" (Jer. 29:11). His plans have been unexpected—healing, comforting, good, slow-developing, never early and never too late, rooted in His love for me and Beatrice. They have been best for me, once I was open to receiving them.

Bats, Mushrooms, and Split Pea Soup
Wonderfully Made

2002–2021

Beatrice loved bats. She had a favorite toy bat. She even wanted to marry one . . . when she was five years old. She also wanted to install a bat house, so she could see the bats come and go. They fascinated her throughout her life. She enjoyed mushrooms though not necessarily for eating. She enjoyed photographing them atop various objects. And her favorite soup was the split pea soup from our neighborhood French restaurant. It was a seasonal soup I wish they had made more often. I know she did. She always ordered it when it was available.

She loved quirky places. When we visited Canada one summer, she found a restaurant that served dinner in complete darkness. The wait staff were all blind.

While I was claustrophobic at first and grew to truly enjoy the experience, Beatrice loved it from the very moment she stepped into the darkness. She was in her element. We ordered before going into the darkened dining area. We could order specific dishes or be surprised. Beatrice chose to be surprised for each course, including dessert. Someone even broke out in song.

She enjoyed kayaking. We did not do it much as a family, but when we did, it became a favorite. We were supposed to kayak during her last visit to Oregon, the last time I saw her alive. We had made reservations though the day before they canceled on us, citing "cold" temperatures and "drizzles" expected the next day. The river is wet! It was June! Wimps! For a family hardened to northeast coast climates, we would have done it in the middle of winter if possible. Kayaking in heaven?

Beatrice was wonderfully made. The things that fascinated her were many—unique to her but shared with others. She brought a richness to life to all of us, exposing us to things we might never consider but that she gravitated toward. I have tried to remember all these unique memories. They were all surprises and all wonderful. Whether it was her extensive tea collection, volumes of *Magic Tree House* books, or the recreation of Solomon's temple and all the artifacts we made as part of her middle school history project—all were part of her uniqueness. The psalmist's words come to mind: "For you created my inmost being; you knit me together in my mother's womb. I praise you because I am fearfully and wonderfully made; your works are wonderful, I know that full well" (Ps. 139:13–14). It is easy for me to slide into familiar and comfortable patterns. I think I need to make a habit of trying the quirky, the unique, the unexpected, and the adventurous. To see a world I may not otherwise experience but one Beatrice would have loved and embraced. A list is already forming in my head. I look forward to telling her what I saw.

Darkness
and the Light of the World
Take Your Time

December 2021

I was back in Oregon. It had been a few weeks since saying good-bye to Beatrice, if saying good-bye only once was ever enough, and I was at church that Sunday morning. We started singing a song with the lyrics "light of the world" in its stanza. Though I was weak emotionally and turned inward, I wanted to prove to myself I could still raise my hands to my Lord and sing in faith, even if everything hurt. With arms extended and a trembling voice, a vision, like a great movie scene etched to memory, appeared. God had given me a vision.

In that vision, I saw layer after layer of darkness pass before my eyes and placed on top of each other. I also saw a thesaurus suspended in air, the size of a larger TV screen, with an extensive list of synonyms for the word *dark*. As each layer of darkness passed before me, I was required to name that layer with one of the descriptors that reflected its darkness, until I ran out of words to describe each layer. The layers were of different materials, thickness, and density. There was even a layer like a swirling thick fog, dark as coal. Next, I saw the "light of the world" (John 8:12), shining in all His brilliance, though I did not see His face. He was shining on the darkness below. Between His radiant light and the dark layers was a brilliant blue expanse, sharp as any cloudless sky I have ever seen in my life.

The dark layers were covering my heart, and the work to remove them was beyond reason, as if a solitary man could reduce a mountain to rubble with a single pick during his lifetime. Even if I were inclined to start, I had no energy to take on this daunting task. However, I got the sense from the Holy Spirit that, over time, Jesus would eventually remove each layer off my heart. There was no need to hurry or panic. It was OK that I dwelled in darkness; it was appropriate for this season of sorrow. His light would eventually prevail!

Grieving takes time, a lot of time; God's process of healing is slow. I wish for normalcy, and yet there is no normal to return to anymore. Grief has utterly displaced me in life. I do not expect anything to be the same, nor do I want to return to the same. Though I hope my loss will never define me, I was hurting, and I wanted to be in that place for as long as possible. It seemed inconceivable to me to feel any joy at that moment when my heart had been ripped out. All I wanted to do was stare into the abyss, stunned and shocked and ambivalent about life. I take heart in knowing my grief process did not need to be rushed by me nor by any other person. I only needed to go at His perfect speed, "He tends his flock like a shepherd: He gathers the lambs in his arms and carries them close to his heart; he gently leads those that have young" (Isa. 40:11).

Geronimo Stilton
God Never Forgets a Precious Memory

Summer 2007

The *Rodent Gazette*! Geronimo Stilton was the publisher and went on amazing adventures all over the world on behalf of his job. Beatrice loved the stories of this mouse and his adventures. So did I. Beatrice loved to read and loved to have me read these stories to her. We spent many nights reading in bed before we said prayers and she went off to sleep. We collected them for many years.

After purchasing every book and reading them, we had to wait for the newest release. We always preordered and waited expectantly for a new adventure that awaited us. The book's author also started publishing additional series based on key characters of the book, such as Geronimo's sister, Thea. We read those as well.

This was one of many fun things Beatrice and I loved to do together as father and daughter. At some point the collection of these books stopped as she grew older. It was a precious moment of her youth, and I loved it! It is a memory I hope I will never forget and celebrate each year.

The all-knowing God. I am anxious about the preservation of memories of her. Her face and voice are even now fading from my memory. I look at photos and listen to the sound of her voice in videos to help me remember. I am afraid I will forget Beatrice's life the more time goes by and do not want to forget my most precious memories. Now that Beatrice is gone, I wish I had saved a handful of those books. I lament over not preserving some of those books but nothing can be done to get them back. I guess I could say that about other areas of her life. How do you hold onto something so dear to your heart when the passage of time crushes your best efforts? I am reminded of a beautiful and deeply comforting psalm that deals with God's ever-presence. It could have easily been written to describe His unlimited power to accomplish all His heart's desires or attest to His complete knowledge of all things, including every memory I have of Beatrice.

Where shall I go from your Spirit?
> Or where shall I flee from your presence?
If I ascend to heaven, you are there!
> If I make my bed in Sheol, you are there!
If I take the wings of the morning
> and dwell in the uttermost parts of the sea,
even there your hand shall lead me,
> and your right hand shall hold me.
If I say, "Surely the darkness shall cover me,
> and the light about me be night,"
even the darkness is not dark to you;
> the night is bright as the day,
> for darkness is as light with you.
>> (Ps. 139:7–12, ESV)

His eternal memory will never allow a memory I have of Beatrice to disappear. He does not forget! (See Isa. 49:15–16.) God has preserved every moment of her life. Though with passing days, these memories may one day lie forgotten by me, lost in the shadows of age and unable to be recalled. However, I don't think I will fear that day. He remembers and can always remind me. After all, He has done so without fail during this first year. I just hope not to forget that He remembers.

A Theology Giant
Children of God

Fall 2007

"Why did God create us?" The little eyes of my young daughter were looking up at me, waiting for a simple answer to her question. *"How do I explain such a complicated question to a five-year-old child?"* I thought to myself. As I contemplated my response, Beatrice said, "I think he wanted to have children," and she turned around and walked away. I stood amazed and silent. "Lord, was that question for me or was that answer for me?" She was correct! Sometimes the answers to the great questions of life and the theological muses boil down to simple answers. In this case, the theological summation of my daughter's questions condensed to one single purpose: God wanted a family.

The family I once had has been shattered and torn in ways that seem to expand with each passing day. The reverberations of grief spread far and wide. They send casting waves onto shores unknown and undesired but must be explored, nevertheless. My role as a father to Beatrice is now over. It is an unknown and undesired shore! How is that even possible? It is hard to fathom that I cannot see her life unfold, but instead it has ended. My memories have been locked in place, never to be moved for my departed child.

I always thought Beatrice might become a theologian. At a young age, she asked deep and astonishing questions about God, and her thoughts were profound and insightful. A deep well of wisdom and understanding flowed from this young and deeply intelligent child. As she approached her later high school years and colleges were being considered, I began praying she would attend Gordon College, a Christian school located in Massachusetts, north of Boston and minutes from the Atlantic Ocean. The school was only several miles from Gordon Conwell, the seminary I attended later in my life. Beatrice ultimately picked another school to attend, but I continued to pray that eventually she would attend Gordon. Her death brought an end to that dream.

The perfect Father. During the two winter months I spent on the East Coast in 2022 to grieve her death, I happened to pass Gordon College while attending a grief group. It was an unexpected stop on my trip, but one my heavenly Father had arranged for me. I pulled into the campus and drove around, parking in various places. I pondered what might have been and thanked God for the opportunity to be on the campus. It was a time of grief and closure, a time to reflect and honor her memory, a time to smile and remember my young theologian, whose knowledge of God has eclipsed mine as she now sees Him "face to face" (1 Cor. 13:12, ESV). He truly is the perfect Father! He knew what my heart needed at that very moment and led me to the place that provided closure and healing of the theological dream for Beatrice.

A Letter in the Mail
The God of All Comfort

December 2021

I was sitting through a grief group during the first month after Beatrice died. I was new to the group and shared my story. I told them that though the Lord had carried me the first few weeks after Beatrice died and spoke to my heart at the time, His comfort was quite absent now. Where was God?

The Bible is clear about God's comfort during times of troubles as Paul wrote to the Corinthian church: "Praise be to the God and Father of our Lord Jesus Christ, the Father of compassion and the God of all comfort, who comforts us in all our troubles, so that we can comfort those in any trouble with the comfort we ourselves receive from God" (2 Cor. 1:3–4). Paul's thoughts continue for several more sentences. I knew this verse well, but there I was sitting without a trace of heavenly support. I was alone now. Where was the God of all comfort? Why did I have to wrestle and plead with Him to carry me in such tragic circumstances?

I headed home. No comfort. No hope of comfort. I stopped at the post office to pick up my mail. There was a letter in it from some dear friends. I waited till I got home to read it. It sat on the kitchen countertop for about an hour before I opened it. I cried as the first printed words of the card hit my heart: "God will tenderly comfort you . . . . He will give you the strength to endure." It was referring to 2 Corinthians 1:7. The handwritten note from the wife was, "May Jesus give you visions of your daughter now, free, healed and full of glory." The God of all comfort had not abandoned me.

The card had been postmarked five days earlier! He had seen me in this future moment and sent a card to comfort me when I arrived home that day in December. I did not know it at the time, but there were a lot of desolate mountainous trails I needed to explore in order to heal. This was one of them. As the first year of life without my daughter had unfolded, an ache appeared in my heart and had grown in intensity. It is repulsive to me. The rips and tears of death and finality are hideous. There is no beauty and hope in their presence. It is an offensive scourge that plagues my thoughts. I have been assured by others it will lessen in time. I wonder if that is true.

The God of all comfort. The God of all comfort has a strange way of caring for the grieving. The temporary reminder in December has given way to a relentless yearning for something more profound and deep to heal this sharp and penetrating wound. A song started to play in my head during this time, and I played it often on my phone. The words soothed my ache. It taught me something that bothered me profoundly yet encouraged me in my vulnerability. In a world of pain, trials, and heartache, He knows that nothing in this world—no matter how appealing, whether human or something else—can truly satisfy my ache, apart from Him. It led me naturally to this conclusion: somehow in sorrow, in the darkest valley of my anguish, the eternal God—my Creator and Father of all, who can touch my cheeks and wipe away the drops of sadness—becomes the One I am truly aching to see and to experience His presence and closeness.

The Baboon Who
Lives in the Tall Grass
Giggles and Laughs

July 2008

S ummer 2008 we celebrated my maternal grandma's ninetieth birthday. Her entire family had gathered in Oregon's high-desert, family-resort community of Sunriver. On the west side, you look upward to the snow-capped cascade mountains, home of Mount Bachelor and the Three Sisters. Douglas fir trees are far and wide. The ground is covered in pine needles, pinecones, and fragments of volcanic rock cast along like bird seed. The Deschutes River forms a windy border around the outer skirts of the community with minimal development, so all the resort's residents and guests can experience the full pleasure of this river. At the time, the mornings were cool and crisp. The days warmed fast with hot afternoons. The setting sun brought back cool and pleasant evenings. The stars at night were beyond measure and bright and crisp, not dimmed by city lights. The very air of the place rejuvenated the spirit with the promise of wholeness. Beatrice was only six years old at the time.

Our rental homes were all along one of the two resort golf courses. The days were filled with new adventures and the evenings with family dinners and long walks. During one of those fun days, we had gathered along the golf course. There were pockets of tall bunchgrass, a common landscape feature in this area of Oregon, near one of the tee boxes. Beatrice spotted one of these and hid inside. As we watched her, she popped her head up in a slow motion, saying "Ooh . . . the baboon who lives in the tall grass." Then slowly she shrank back into the tall grass to hide herself once again. Up she came again, "Ooh, the baboon who lives in the tall grass." Then down she went! The laughter and giggles filled the air as this curly-haired imp with a wild smile and twinkling eyes bobbed up and down.

Laugher and heartache. In one way this memory is wonderful, delightful, playful, whimsical. In another way it has become bitter because she is no more. We can never laugh about that moment together. It has been lost on this earth forever. Though the memory is sweet and adds a smile to my face, it is stained in bitterness. It is not that the memory itself is bitter, but death is bitter and tarnishes and brings shadows and darkness to everything it touches. I despise bitterness' presence in this memory, and I can't imagine it becoming a sweet memory again apart from my daughter's presence. Yet I am strangely drawn to the cross in this moment: "After he has suffered, he will see the light of life and be satisfied" (Isa. 53:11). Over the course of three days, the bitterness of a shredded body, a bloody cross, and a dark grave gave way to the sweet aroma of an empty tomb. Perhaps nailing this memory and other memories to His cross might produce a similar outcome. I will nail it in death and wait for a resurrected, sweet memory, debittered in His precious blood (see 1 Pet. 1:19), emerging in new life. One day I will be able to laugh but not right now.

Blankie

Abandoned and Lonely

March 2002–November 2021

The green Beatrix Potter–inspired blanket that was part of Beatrice's infant bed set was named Blankie. Blankie first belonged to my oldest daughter and was given to Beatrice when she came into this world. It was Beatrice's companion throughout her life. Whenever we traveled, Blankie was packed with her luggage and was one of the items on our pre-trip checklist before departing. I do not recall ever leaving Blankie behind. It traveled through many states and even went as far as Paris, France, and Glacier Bay National Park in Alaska. Blankie was cherished.

As the years went by, this beloved comfort became frayed, and the stuffing started to fall out. To preserve Blankie, we decided to encase it in a pillowcase. Each night Beatrice fell asleep with her beloved blanket next to her head or wrapped in her arms. I am sure it was the most loved and washed item in our household. It was her security blanket. Now it's a treasured keepsake!

I have other treasured items from her life I am preserving. The list is small though quite meaningful. I am not sure what we will ultimately do with Blankie. It is hard to make such decisions, and I don't want to be rash about something that can never be undone. It will take time to decide, and I am not in a hurry to make any decisions of how best to honor and preserve this memory. It is quite possible Blankie will be preserved throughout my lifetime.

Blankie remains on earth alone and abandoned. It should not be this way. It is hard to comprehend. As months of the first year passed, I also experienced a foreboding and ominous loneliness, like the shadows of a setting sun. Like the October coastal fogs that come unexpectedly fast in Oregon, it engulfed my heart and mind. *Turning to family and friends will certainly soothe the shadowy dread*, I thought. It made it worse and grew in intensity as I spent time with them. I had no interest in this type of life. I was alarmed and knew this was not a path to travel.

Alone. Perhaps it was Jesus drawing me into a much deeper relationship. I hoped so because this was not sustainable if this was how life was going to unfold.

I carved out time to focus on Him and inquired about what was going on in my life that would cause such loneliness. It was in quite an unpleasant way that my real need emerged: "It is not good for the man to be alone" (Gen. 2:18). My deep loneliness was really a deep yearning for a mate, an intimate friend, confidant, and partner. Someone to share the rest of my life. I did not need her to mend a broken heart—Jesus was doing that—but someone to share an adventure with God. Still, it did not seem right to think about such things during that first year. However, it did pull me out of dwelling on the immovable past and place my eyes on the possible present. I did not need to feel guilty about wanting to enjoy life again nor shut myself off from risking loss. God, in His goodness, had picked someone for me and me for her. I think I will pray for her while I wait for the day to be revealed.

The Redwoods
Was There No Other Way?

February 2022 to December 2022

"Father, why did you take my child?" Why did I even have to ask such a question? I was warned by those with experience in matters of loss and grief not to expect an answer. That seemed reasonable. Job was never told why his life was uprooted and destroyed. Besides, what possible answer would even make sense when the only happy outcome was no longer possible? Beatrice was dead.

I did seek out the thoughts of two trusted friends. I knew they would help provide some possible explanation. Both had a similar thought though they came at it from different directions. Both answers were a comfort to me, removing the intensity of needing an immediate answer. While the question is natural to ask, a more profound and deeper question emerged that needed an answer. That question emerged during a session with a therapist.

I was two months into the grieving process, and I broke down at work. I decided to go on an extended leave of absence, which ultimately lasted seven months. I used this time to grieve and get answers from the Lord about what happened. During the first week, I did a mental exercise with my therapist that helped me calm down. I imagined a safe place and invited Jesus to enter that place. I loved the Redwoods located along the northern California coast and hiked there often. I imagined all my favorite places with me in the midst of them. I was lost in my imagination when my therapist said, "Now invite Jesus into your scene." I had been lost in my thoughts and forgot we were going to do that. I broke down crying and turned to Him and asked Him two questions, "Why did you take my daughter? Was there no other way?" I was too weak to even listen to an answer if one were provided. I was not strong nor courageous enough to hear the answer. What could He possibly say?

Reflecting on the encounter, the first question seemed a natural response of any grieving parent. The second question was a surprise. I eventually realized this was a question He gave me to ask Him. There would be an answer, though not one I expected nor ever anticipated. It took months for an answer to emerge, not all at once but in pieces and culminating in my last session with the same therapist a few days before Christmas 2022.

"Was there no other way?" I assumed the question meant no other way was possible that involved Beatrice living and not dying. I couldn't accept that answer. His omnipotence makes that impossible. There is always another way. Was this God's best? Again, I cringe at even thinking this could be the case. Each successive question caused me to frown, for the implications seemed repulsive to me, and there must have been a better way. It wasn't until I realized that Jesus had asked the same question of His Father as it concerned the cross that I had a place to explore for an answer. At the same time, the cross seemed so grotesque to me. A needless and heartless death. Yet the cross was not forced upon Jesus. He chose that loathsome cross freely for my sake. My freedom He secured. The one my heart longs for had rescued me, for He loved me deeply. He was kind and tender toward me. I will never experience the second death, for He has given me eternal life (see the books of John and Revelations). The One who put the question on my heart to ask had Himself faced the same question before His Father.

The answer I sought had two branches that intersected, the nature of God and the plight of man. One branch reflected my Father's underlying nature, reflected to me through His Son. He is good, kind, tender, and loving in everything He does. The second branch was my ongoing predicament: I am broken, living in a broken world, and will one day die.

I hate to admit this because I selfishly desire my daughter's life on this earth, to see it unfold, to spend days talking with her and seeing her and her family. Yet quite reluctantly I must acknowledge she is not mine. She was never mine, even though for a time it seemed that way. She was a gift. I want to hold onto this life as if it will last forever and so my heart never hurts. It is unrealistic. It is inevitable that both Beatrice and I would die. I just didn't want to witness her death. However, it would have come nevertheless, apart from the return of our King. If she had lived longer, she would have witnessed my passage. One of us was going to weep and mourn. It was as inevitable as day and night.

I also know well the struggle I endure each day I am left in this broken world. The struggle against my own fleshly desires that are contrary to God's goodness, the prevalent evil ways of this world that landscape too many aspects of my life, and the ongoing attacks by my enemy, Satan, with his demonic gang tagging along. Beatrice faced the same struggle, yet the Lord saw it was more than He was willing to allow her to experience and allowed her to come home to Him. He could have intervened, and she would be with us today. He chose what was best for Beatrice, not to inflict pain and grief on her and on those who loved her but to spare her the evil days ahead. God saw Beatrice's deep pain and suffering, and His mercy and kindness to Beatrice brought her home. Paul put it this way:

> For we know that if the tent that is our earthly home is destroyed, we have a building from God, a house not made with hands, eternal in the heavens. For in this tent we groan, longing to put on our heavenly dwelling, if indeed by putting it on we may not be found naked. For while we are still in this tent, we groan, being burdened—not that we would be unclothed, but that we would be further clothed, so that what is mortal may be swallowed up by life. He who has prepared us for this very thing is God, who has given us the Spirit as a guarantee.
>
> So we are always of good courage. We know that while we are at home in the body we are

away from the Lord, for we walk by faith, not by sight. Yes, we are of good courage, and we would rather be away from the body and at home with the Lord. So whether we are at home or away, we make it our aim to please him. For we must all appear before the judgment seat of Christ, so that each one may receive what is due for what he has done in the body, whether good or evil. (2 Cor. 5:1–10, ESV)

Her pain is over. Her struggle with her flesh is over. She is free and in His glory. Beatrice is no longer restricted and bound by the limitations of this world. She now sees all of God's extraordinary creation, heaven and earth, as well as her Creator face to face. She now experiences God's perfect will being done every day in heaven. Her tears are no more. She is in paradise with all the servants of God who have left this earth since the creation of this world. She has the freedom to create without hinderances. Her daily existence exceeds mine in every way. It was hard to see at first, but He was displaying His mercy and kindness to me, His servant, as well, who is left to struggle in this broken world and with his own eventual death but who knows the second death will never happen.

Woolly Buffalo
A Weight Unbearable

Spring 2009

Woolly Buffalo, Frog and Flies, and the Blanket Monster were some of the fun games I played with my two daughters when they were young. They were all games I made up, and both girls loved them. Each one produced suspense, excitement, and giggles. I was the monster under the blanket, and the girls were to avoid me even though I tried to trick them and tell them I was harmless. When they drew near, I grabbed them and pretended to eat them.

I was the frog in the circle as each "fly" tried to walk just out of my reach. I leaped out and grabbed my dinner. Any fly caught was "eaten." Those flies were laughing uncontrollably as they were being snacked upon.

I was also the buffalo that tried to buck off each unwanted rider. Everyone went on a rodeo ride before being thrown off safely onto the soft and comfortable couch. We went and went until the buffalo needed a rest. It's a weary thing being a buffalo.

The love of my daughters was sweet and the trust complete. They were young and innocent hearts. Beautiful moments kept secure in my heart, lighthearted and innocent moments! These were the times that brought smiles, when things were young and fresh, the worries of life were few. Times of joy when burdens were light, including the girls who giggled when gobbled.

If only I could return to the days of old. The weight of my loss has grown and affected every other aspect of life. Its reach is beyond comprehension. It seeks out every frayed fragment of light and hope and covers it in blighted darkness. Like molasses or pitch, it seeps down into every crevice and crusts over like cooling molten lava. It leaves an impregnable and impermeable shell where no light nor hope comes and goes without its permission.

It was in this dreaded state God brought up the unwanted thought that something fruitful would come forth out of this loss. I wasn't looking to start over let alone find something meaningful to emerge. I wanted to cling to the hopeful past, the comfortable familiar, the old ways, the wonder of the dreams developed over

Beatrice's lifetime. Now life felt like a favorite book lost at sea and dumped ashore like driftwood, with all the print washed away. Words dear to my heart now replaced with the smell of sea salt and ocean kelp. I now had a life with no reference points in this world apart from one, Jesus. I didn't ask for this. This topic was to be avoided and delayed for as long as possible.

Fruit in dark places. Yes, it was true; I had to start over, and I needed to find something to make a new life. He would make this loss fruitful. I was now a branch with no leaves and no blossoms (see John 15). Yet somehow, He would take this deep loss and one day make it bear fruit. I suppose I can take that old favorite book with the ocean saltwater-washed-out pages and begin the first sentence, "In my valley of the shadow of death, a Light emerged. . . ." I hope it turns out to be a good book.

Thunder Hole,
Arcadia National Park, Maine
Abba, Father!

February 2022

I needed to cry! I needed to scream! It had been three months since Beatrice died, and I was struggling to process the grief. I process stuff analytically, and grief had overwhelmed all my normal faculties for processing the loss of my child. Grief does not fall within that framework. Grief is emotional and physical. Without release, it had built up inside me, like water behind a dam. My other daughter and I had taken a trip to Maine, and we decided to visit Acadia National Park, next to Bar Harbor.

I stood in front of Thunder Hole, a rock feature along the coast, one of the park's main attractions. My oldest daughter had gone for a short walk to give me privacy. I broke down crying. I had never learned to scream properly and now was not the time to learn. I tried twice to make a great and unintelligible roar! My effort to release the surging and swirling waters of sorrow contained within me was completely unsatisfying and embarrassing. I elected to holler out Beatrice's name. "Beatrice!" I shouted as if I was calling her and looking for her. I broke down crying again. I shouted at the top of my voice. I was partly worried people would show up, and so I looked around as often as I shouted. I shouted out, "Jesus!" but felt something was still missing. My heart was still not satisfied. I prayed. "Abba" came immediately to mind, and so I shouted, "Abba! Why did you take my daughter? Where are you, Beatrice? I never had an opportunity to say good-bye!"

The waves continued to roll over the rocks. The tide was out, so only an occasional crash and thunder sound was heard. Blue sky above. Cold, though not bitter, sea air breezed. Finishing up my coffee, I saw ice had formed on the rocks in the distance. The water must be frigid.

Eventually, I made up my mind not to care and shouted once more. Then I turned around and saw several families had now gathered at the top of the stairs, as if an audience had met to hear a rock concert with me playing lead. I am sure they thought I was crazy.

Abba. Abba was the name Jesus used when He pleaded with His Father in the garden asking if there was another way other than the cross to accomplish His Father's redemption of humanity (see Mark 14:36, ESV). The name evokes warmth, intimacy, comfort, safety, and trust. Of all the possible names (Lord, Yahweh) or descriptions (rock, shield) of God, the one that came to mind was the most intimate of names in the darkest moment of Jesus's life. There are deep hurts in life that only Abba can comfort. This is one of them.

Painting
Bridges and Flowers in the Storm

March 2022

I took up painting during my early days of grief. I needed an outlet to process my intense emotions. The owner of the local art store near my place in Ipswich, Massachusetts, was extremely helpful and had me outfitted in less than an hour. I explained why I was buying these paints, and she immediately understood. I think art has a wonderful capacity to heal the heart. I found this true of the psalms as well. In fact, they were the only scriptures that provided any solace for most of the first year of life without Beatrice.

I had a phase in my life several decades ago when I painted, so I was somewhat familiar with how to approach my art. I was not concerned with the aesthetic beauty of what I was working on as much as needing my heart to express its darkness and intense pain on canvas. An inner tempest was quickly destroying me.

Its relentless darkness had been raging for days and nights! A tumultuous storm of emotions and sorrow had overwhelmed my capacity to release my grief. Now my heart had a place to express its silent screams and deep tears.

Each stroke of the brush released a fragment of the intensity of the darkness that had engulfed me. The ocean was my topic. Its powerful, swirling, blue-and-white splattered waves smashing upon lonely rocks was my theme. The waves do not yield to a command, nor will they sit still when the wind howls. The rocks cannot flee to shelter to escape the ocean's turmoil. They were placed, in an age beyond memory, against their will to be pelted again and again. Unending, unrelenting, unsympathetic was the ocean of their condition. These were fierce brush strokes filled with anguish. My hands were instruments to a heart pouring out its turbulence, striking and slashing the canvas with blackened hues of blues and tarnished whites. My sorrow had an outlet.

The paintings were also beautiful. My heart painted the chaos of the ocean. When the intense storm faded, faith painted the flowers and the bridges. One was reckless with the brush. The other was a focused and concentrated effort to paint beauty and stability in the scenes.

Beauty out of ashes. When I look back at my art, I am frightened by what I painted. These were raw emotions, uncontrolled and destructive and crying out in anguish. Nothing in this world could soothe and comfort the hurt. A scream, a cry, a desperate father captured in my art. It was unrefined hurt, void of words and incomprehensible expression. I am startled at the madman who did these things. Yet during these paintings, I yearned for what Jesus could only do: "to comfort all who mourn, and provide for those who grieve in Zion—to bestow on them a crown of beauty instead of ashes, the oil of joy instead of mourning, and a garment of praise instead of a spirit of despair" (Isa. 61:2–3). I had ashes at that time. The beauty has taken awhile to emerge.

Waffles and Sausages
The Sweet Joys of Life

September 2013 and March 2022

The smell and taste of waffles and sausage, any pork in general, were some of Beatrice's favorite foods. These are some of my favorite foods as well, though not in the early months after her death. I had lost my appetite and enjoyment for all foods.

I had to force myself to eat healthy. First, I had to remember to eat. It was necessary but not a pleasure. I wanted something comforting, but the idea of savoring food was repulsive to me. How could I even take pleasure in anything, let alone food, when my daughter was dead? It seemed wrong. Death has a way of shaming the pleasures of life, even things such as a hearty laugh with friends. The sweet joys of life had been stripped of all desire and meaning. Would life ever have any joy and sweetness to it again?

I was told that, as I healed, I would start enjoying life again. It was necessary that I healed. I knew it was important. Living in the shadows of a gray existence is no type of life. However, what does *healing* even mean? Is that even the correct word to use when working through the death of a child? Life was never going to return to normal, so how can *healing* be the correct word?

I am not sure I am ready to enjoy life again. I am not sure I want to leave grief. I am scared to leave it! Where will I go? It is not a season that automatically transitions, and what it transitions into is unclear to me. I am hesitant to depart its company, as I am worried I will be thrown out into a barren world without direction. Grief has become a shelter for me to hide from this painful and unsafe world but one I knew I had to leave. It is unhealthy for me to dwell here too long.

My daughter left an immeasurable impact on my life, and so I do not want to leave grief until I capture all its lessons. I fear most that I will waste this season of heartache. I fear I will forget, ignore, or hide from its lessons and spend the rest of my life in regret because I did not have the courage to look death in the face and allow God to lead me through the darkness. I guess I want to experience the sweet joys of life through a new view of life—one He created for me out of the darkness. Then I will know that life will have meaning again.

The sweet joys of life. During my stay in Massachusetts, I visited Crane Beach, just north of Cape Ann, "a conservation and recreation property that consists of a four-mile-long sandy beachfront, dunes, and a maritime pitch pine forest." The morning sun and the unusual warm spell made quick work of a very cold winter day. The clouds had the day off. The cold dew of the sand was welcomed heartily by my bare feet as I walked the many miles of dune trails and then along the beach. The breeze was light. The youth of my days returned as I enjoyed all the pleasures of a trip to the ocean—wading deep into the ocean, collecting sand dollars, digging up a clam. I even watched seagulls pick up clams and drop them from the sky until their lunch was open and they could feast. All brought me such delight inside. I built sand dams to block little streams going into the ocean. I noticed fear and dread were removed for the day. Gratitude filled my heart. My senses started to recognize life again. I was surprised. Delight filled my heart as did laughter. I smiled as tears formed by a light heart, its warmth returning after an arduous journey. The four long months of carrying the dark weight of the loss was lifted for the day. It was a moment of joy and a break in the grief! It was His idea! It was also a precursor and a reminder from God that the sweet joys and simple pleasures of life would slowly come back and be enjoyed once again. He would see to it, "The LORD is close to the brokenhearted and saves those who are crushed in spirit" (Ps. 34:18). That day and His promise was a reassuring comfort to me!

Psalm 121
A Father's Prayer

Spring 2016

I prayed the words of Psalm 121 over Beatrice's life with great regularity and devotion. I inserted her name into each line of the psalm as I prayed it back to God. I had it almost memorized. The psalm is precious to me, for the Lord gave it to me, placing it on my heart, to cover Beatrice in His loving care and protection. The psalm immediately recalls many memories and God's faithfulness over her years. I have never doubted He fulfilled every word even though she died so early in life. It is beautiful and wonderful to me.

> I lift up my eyes to the mountains—
>> where does my help come from?
> My help comes from the LORD,
>> the Maker of heaven and earth.

He will not let your foot slip—
    he who watches over you will not slumber;
indeed, he who watches over Israel
    will neither slumber nor sleep.
The LORD watches over you—
    the LORD is your shade at your right hand;
the sun will not harm you by day,
    nor the moon by night.
The LORD will keep you from all harm—
    he will watch over your life;
the LORD will watch over your coming and going
    both now and forevermore. (Ps. 121)

The privilege of a praying father. It was a privilege to pray for my child. The time with God, to talk with Him about her, was a delight and wonderful experience. I tried to peer into her future to see what would unfold, to see how best to pray for her, to see what God had planned for her life, and how best to respond as a father. I was faithful to pray for my child each day of her life. Sometimes I spent a long time meditating on her life in prayer. I know I did this one thing well during all her days. She was dear to my heart, and my prayers were a reflection of my love for her. I no longer need to pray for her. She is in the presence of the great I

Am. She is snug in His embrace now. Though each time I come across the psalm, I smile. It was His psalm for her. I had the privilege to pray it back to Him. "Thank You, Father!"

Winter in New Hampshire
My Mortality

March 2022

My daughter's death forced me to deal with my own mortality. It was in the White Mountains of New Hampshire on a bitter-cold March weekend that this unpleasant topic emerged. Snow and ice covered the town of Lincoln, a population of two thousand, and the nearby Flume Gorge in Franconia Notch State Park. My surroundings were beautiful though isolated and austere. An idyllic retreat from any metropolis as your soul breathes deeply of God's rugged creation. Yet for me, it was quite a lonely and desolate place. It was not what I had expected. It was, however, the perfect location for what God had planned to teach me that weekend.

I arrived in the afternoon to a canopy of grayish-white winter clouds. A snowstorm was in the works for the next day. With the light I had remaining in the day, I explored Lincoln and the gorge. Dinner included a delicious steak, potatoes, and mixed vegetables. The hotel I was staying in was nice, though it lacked the crackling fire and hot chocolate atmosphere that would complement the brutal coldness outside. The next day, the snow arrived, and the visibility to drive was nonexistent. All snowmobiles were rented for the day. I was thus cooped up all day apart from walking to the local breakfast joint, the wind hindering each step and the falling snow using me as a mold for a snowman.

It was under these circumstances when the Lord and I, His very reluctant child, explored my own eventual death. Prompted by a book I was reading on the topic of loss and grief, I was now at the chapter that focused on how the death of those we love forces us to reckon with our own mortality. My eventual death had always been an abstract concept to me, something that will happen sometime in the way distant future. It was a hypothetical thing that could be delayed serious thought. It had popped up from time to time, but I was young, and it wasn't urgent to truly consider it. No need to acknowledge something so dreadful and final. Beatrice's death brought an end to the illusion, the hypothetical, and the procrastination. I was now locked up with death in an icy and harsh environment. A storm raged outside, matching the storm inside.

The Lord had chosen a season of the year and a place where life is barren and dark. If a garden were to be planted on this day, it would die, encased in a frosty tomb. Wistful thoughts of spring and summer obliterated by the relentless pressure of the wind against my window and the rising layers of snow. I will die. This monstrous topic could no longer be delayed. It is a dreadful reality that I will one day no longer feel the warmth of the sun, feel the breeze on my face, hear the laughs of my oldest daughter, or speak to my friends. What a sharp and bitter truth. How do I align my life now to this ugly reality? How can my life just cease? Beatrice's life did and mine will also! Death is repulsive. Why should this be so?

This is my Father's world. I was in anguish and distress, and Jesus's words soothed my soul that day: "Come to Me, all you who are weary and burdened, and I will give you rest. Take My yoke upon you and learn from Me, for I am gentle and humble in heart, and you will find rest for your souls. For My yoke is easy and My burden is light" (Matt. 11:28–30, NASB1995). Then the story of the crucifixion started to permeate my thoughts. I wrote down two of its implications. First,

Jesus has the power to heal my broken heart. Second, He loves me. For the moment, fear was quenched, and another truth emerged through shadows of fear. Though this world is decaying, and I will one day die, this is still my Father's world. The ownership has not changed. The haunting specter of death need not hold its sway over my heart. Fear need not cloud my future in a world my Father has made and who encourages me to explore it, look around every corner, and embrace the adventure He has laid out for me without fear or reservations!

The Ride
A Time to Grieve

March 2022

The sweet and happy place of Hershey, Pennsylvania! Located a little more than two hours away from our home in New Jersey, this "sweetest place on earth" was a favorite family vacation designation. The air in Hershey was saturated with the smells of cocoa! Heaven for a chocolate-craved family like ours. The town contained some of our favorite sites, restaurants, an amusement park, and our favorite destination of all: Hershey's Chocolate Tour inside of Hershey's Chocolate World. This free chocolate factory tour ride takes you on "a delicious journey from tropical cocoa bean to wrapped candy bar . . . feel the warmth of roasting cocoa beans, smell rich milk chocolate and watch thousands of candies twist and turn on conveyor belts." We called it, "The Ride!"

The selling point for us was the "delight your tastebuds with a sweet product sample at the end!" Our record for completing the Ride during one vacation stay was seven times. Each time eating a delicious candy bar. Yum! It satisfied our sweet tooths, and it was a wonderful way to begin the day or relax from a busy day. At the end of the ride, guests posed for a souvenir photo, available for purchase. We did funny family poses each time we rode through it. When the children were young, my wife and I picked each up by the legs and dangled them upside or sideways. We purchased that photo as a family keepsake. I believe it was the only photo we ever purchased.

During the two months I traveled the East Coast grieving and revisiting family memories, I stopped by Hershey to ride the Ride. I reflected on all the memories I had of our trips to Hershey and everything else God brought to my mind. I took some photos of the cows and other fun displays along the ride. I smiled as I reminisced, enjoying this ride for the last time. As I neared the end, the photo place came into view. I prepared myself and smiled. Flash! I purchased that photo as a keepsake. I gave it to my oldest daughter.

I ordered myself a vanilla ice cream with dark chocolate sauce before leaving Chocolate World and watched the *Willy Wonka and the Chocolate Factory* remake that night. Everything I did was to honor the memory of Beatrice and relive a chocolate moment. The one attribute about my daughter that stood out the most during that day was her kindness. She was sweet!

A time to grieve and heal. Ecclesiastes tells us, "There is a time for everything, and a season for every activity under the heavens: a time to be born and a time to die, . . . a time to kill and a time to heal, . . . a time to weep and a time to laugh, a time to mourn and a time to dance" (Eccles. 3:1–4). This was my time to enter into every important memory I had of Beatrice, our family, and our time together—and remember, honor, and grieve what will never happen again "under the sun" (Eccles. 1:3). Hershey was one of many powerful reminders of my loss, and I needed to go into each of them, not knowing ahead of time what would occur. It would have been easy to avoid these places, but I needed to experience the pain, remember my precious, and honor her life. In the end I found rest for my soul!

Dell's Lemonade
A Gift of Grace

March 2022

The Breakers, built with the vast wealth of the Vanderbilt railroad dynasty, is one of many late-nineteenth-century mansions carefully preserved by the Newport Historical Society located in Newport, Rhode Island. I first visited these summer getaways as a child, then with my wife while we were dating, and then with our children. These time capsules of opulent wealth and lavish lifestyles of America's richest families, as well as the city itself, became a favorite and frequent destination of our family during the summer and held special memories. It was also on my list of important stops to remember and honor my memories of Beatrice during my time on the East Coast. I spent two days in Newport.

I knew I needed to go to Newport, but at the same time, I was scared and anxious. How was I to honor these memories? So I asked God what I should do while I was there. His plan was quite simple: eat at Tony's Crab Shack, visit the mansions, grab a dozen donuts from Ma's Donuts, and pick up Dell's Lemonade to take back to New Jersey to celebrate Beatrice's birthday. All these things were family favorites. I could now enter each memory without anxiety because God had picked my itinerary. I also grabbed a souvenir for my oldest daughter from the Mable House mansion's gift shop, something decorated with a pineapple theme.

Finding the lemonade was a miracle. The drink was regional to New England (occasionally we found it in New Jersey) and should have been easy to find. However, for reasons unknown, the stores stopped carrying it in the Newport area. Tony's had also stopped selling it months ago. This was Beatrice's favorite lemonade. It was an important part of my memories of her in this place. I had to find it, no matter how far I had to travel! As I asked the cashier at Tony's where I might look next, he remembered they may have some leftover supply in the back room. After checking with the store manager, he brought out four bottles! The Lord had saved them for me. A miracle gift for a very difficult stop.

I will not be overwhelmed. God remembers the most prized traditions and moments of our vacations to Newport. He led me into this place and prepared everything so I could grieve and cherish her memory. Nothing was lacking, and things were kept aside for me for that moment in time! He knows my hurt and pain and guides me through the healing process. I am reminded of the word of God given to Isaiah to encourage the Israelites: "But now, this is what the Lord says—he who created you, Jacob, he who formed you, Israel: 'Do not fear, for I have redeemed you; I have summoned you by name; you are mine. When you pass through the waters, I will be with you; and when you pass through the rivers, they will not sweep over you. When you walk through the fire, you will not be burned; the flames will not set you ablaze" (Isa. 43:1–2). A lemonade toast to you, my precious child!

March 30
The God Who Plans Birthday Parties

March 2022

Beatrice was born on March 30, 2002. The first birthday after her death was a day I was dreading. How do I celebrate the day and honor my daughter's memory? The anxiety weighed heavy on my heart. There were so many memories to honor. How would I ever fit everything in? And what if it wasn't healing but instead brought greater sadness and darkness into my life? How should I incorporate my other daughter, my former wife, into this day?

As I was driving through Virginia to stay overnight in a town on the outskirts of Shenandoah National Park, the plan emerged. It was a simple plan the Lord gave to me. Simple yet filled with deep and emotional meaning. Perfect for the day. There were only four memories to focus on. The stress and anxiety I was feeling was replaced with a meaningful and structured plan for this day. I knew I would be able to both freely mourn and treasure my daughter's birthday. I could enter the day with courage and allow my emotions and thoughts to flow fully without worrying that I was missing something significant—something I would later regret I had not done. You only get one opportunity at this moment. This was my mindset. You want to capture everything you need to do on that day and not have any regrets because you forgot something. I have learned, since then, that the Lord can find ways to capture moments over several days and leaves behind no regrets.

I was staying at a local bed and breakfast and started my first celebration of her birthday by visiting the hospital where she was born. I walked around the hospital and went up to the nursery reception area and sat in the waiting area, meditating on her life. From there, I went to the cafeteria, where I had gotten breakfast the day she was born and drank my coffee while looking at one of the photos I had of her. I placed it on the table where I was sitting. Just looking at her.

After a few hours at the hospital, I picked up a cake at Natale's Bakery in Summit and had her name engraved on a chocolate disc to display on top. Natale's was our favorite bakery and our number one source for birthday cakes, apart from making them ourselves. This was the second precious memory on the list. My oldest daughter and former wife shared the cake with me the following day. Each of us had our own way of mourning and remembering Beatrice on that day. I may have taken a slice that night, but I don't remember. I had purchased the cake on her day and that was good enough for me.

The third memory followed immediately after the cake purchase. I went to the local bookstore and purchased one of the Geronimo Stilton books we had read together in her youth. I read the book later that night after dinner at Lorena's Restaurant, the fourth and final memory.

Lorena's was our family's favorite restaurant. We went to it on special occasions only, especially birthdays. We always went at least once, if not twice, a year. The exquisite French cuisine, ambiance, and service made this restaurant a treat and delightful time. The waiter asked if I wanted him to prepare a place setting for Beatrice. I thanked him for such a kind gesture and said yes. Though I had not initially planned this, I ended up ordering everything Beatrice would have ordered.

I started the night with Beatrice's and my favorite drink and lifted my glass up to heaven to honor her. They had a dessert special, which was the first time in my life I remember them having a dessert special. It was a lemon tart. The memories came flooding back of the time Beatrice accidentally made the best dessert ever in our household, a lemon tart. She misread the recipe and ended up making something truly exceptional. Lorena's lemon tart special was the Lord's doing, and so I ordered it. He even planned down to the dessert and the wonderful memory it triggered. The day was better than I could have ever imagined or planned on my own. My heavenly Father knew my memories and orchestrated everything I needed to celebrate and mourn my daughter's birthday. I can only imagine her birthday party in heaven.

God can be trusted with the details! God was much better at planning the details than I could be. He had so many unexpected surprises that day. I am eternally grateful. He was in charge and knew everything important to do. Between these four memories, I ended up visiting other places from Beatrice's youth. I sat in those places and allowed the memories to flow in. I eventually realized the Lord was taking me on a path that would provide some measure of closure to certain areas of our shared lives. I asked whether I should visit any other places, and one more was given to me. I just sat in that parking lot looking at the place that played a large role in our family's life and once again allowed memories to flood in and mourn them. Once I left, I had the closure I needed in large areas of life. These were the ones my heavenly Father picked for me, and they were healing, including lunch at a favorite diner where I ordered one of Beatrice's favorites, an egg salad sandwich. It was delicious. There was one other unexpected gift. Her death did bring an end to the bitterness my former wife and I had toward one another and strangely brought healing and friendship. Something we both needed, my oldest daughter craved, and the Lord worked out. He has a mysterious and redemptive way to mend all the broken pieces of our lives.

A Struggling Mother
A Tender Spirit

Summer 2011 and April 2022

Ispotted her as I pulled into the gym. Her face was familiar; immediately she reminded me of my daughter Beatrice. She was clearly living on the streets. I saw her pick up a bottle and smash it on the parking area, glass went everywhere. I saw a young woman who was angry and disappointed in her life, and my heart immediately went out to her. As I wondered what I should do next, she walked away. I picked up the glass, not wanting any of the other cars to suffer a flat tire. Then I went to catch up with her, but she was gone. I finished my workout and went to look for her again. I did this for several days hoping to find her. Finally, I prayed, "Lord, if you want me to find her, you need to make it obvious to me." A week later as I parked at the gym and was getting out of the car, I spotted her sitting on the sidewalk. I approached her, and we talked for a while. She was a struggling mother, trying her best to pick up the broken pieces.

That encounter with a young mother reminded me of a quality I have admired in Beatrice. Her tenderness. Beatrice saw the hurt in others. She had a tender spirit and instinctively gravitated to the neglected, the unwanted, and the brokenhearted. Her heart instantly picked up the fractures in others that could easily go unnoticed. To her it was an opportunity to comfort others, and she always knew what was best to soothe a soul. It seemed she had an endless reservoir of tenderness, fed from the streams and rivers of God to a troubled heart.

My mother-in-law had been wheelchair bound for several years as a result of a stroke when tragedy struck her heart again the day after Christmas 2010. Her husband was rushed to the hospital and never regained the ability to speak. He died at the start of the new year. She was soon moved to her new retirement home. She had lost her ability to walk, her husband, and her home. Her soul filled with grief and despair. During the summer of that year, Beatrice asked to do a sleepover with her grandma. It was a temporary joy for a grandma who had been dealt bitter blows, and it lifted her spirits. This is what Beatrice did best, lift the spirits of others.

Beatrice's life had meaning. I didn't want her death to be a date in the past but something that would bear fruit in the future. Something good and redemptive had to come out of this loss. It couldn't just be over. The story of the woman at the well kept coming to mind (see John 4:1–42). Jesus had encountered the most broken woman in a Samaritan community, and within a few minutes, her life was fully restored. Every life is precious, and to lend a hand in helping others experience the type of redemption that woman at the well experienced seemed good and redemptive to me. I've learned to see more of what Beatrice saw during her life. My heart picks up more quickly on the cracks in people's lives. I seek them out more than in the past. People's losses and brokenness once frightened me because I thought I needed to somehow help in the healing process yet did not know how. I learned through my own journey that others cannot heal wounds; it is Christ who does the mending. I also discovered I could offer to others a part of Beatrice's legacy—a tender heart, a listening ear, friendship, and a willingness to serve. I hope I do her honor.

Easter
He Is Risen Indeed!

April 2022

He is risen! Why does this sound so hollow? How does it get my daughter back? What difference does it make? My daughter was gone, and all I had was the pain of her loss. Easter is supposed to be a hopeful day, but I was empty in spirit. If I was asked the day before if I would expect the day to be meaningful, I would have replied yes. God had been so gracious to me during my journey, guiding me through each difficult moment with His presence and direction. He had prepared each memory and key milestone with something that brought closure and healing. Thus, I fully expected Him to do something meaningful, to bring healing, on my first Easter without Beatrice. Instead, I was hollow, empty inside and unsure of what to make of this day.

My Christian faith rests on the resurrection of Christ. Easter commemorates this essential event. As Paul said, "For if the dead are not raised, then Christ has not been raised either. And if Christ has not been raised, your faith is futile; you are still in your sins" (1 Cor. 15:16–17). Except there was no special revelation, no special meaning attached to this day as it concerned my loss. Why was He not speaking into this day as He had spoken into my other days? I know He listens to me. He knows I needed a special touch of His love on this day. Something to comfort me. Why was this great day hollow?

It has been almost a year since Easter, and I am now questioning Him about that day. I know His voice sometimes lingers until He makes Himself and His reasons known. During this past year, I guess there was so much else to process and be grateful for along the way I chalked it up as only another dark moment, without questioning it much. Now I wanted to know why.

He is risen. I always enjoyed the day, and it had become more meaningful to me in years before Beatrice died. Now I was hollow and perplexed. However, that day was not hollow to His disciples the first Easter. How could it have been? The magnitude and breadth of the consequences of the death of Jesus to their lives was beyond measure. Their hearts had an irreparable tear saved by only one event, which they didn't believe was possible, His resurrection. Peter, now rooted firmly in seeing His friend and Lord alive, was then able to say with beaming joy and personal knowledge, "God has raised this Jesus to life, and we are all witnesses of it. Therefore let all Israel be assured of this: God has made this Jesus, whom you crucified, both Lord and Messiah" (Acts 2:32, 36). His concluding remarks made my hollow heart fill with joy, "Repent and be baptized, every one of you, in the name of Jesus Christ for the forgiveness of your sins. And you will receive the gift of the Holy Spirit. The promise is for you and your children and for all who are far off—for all whom the Lord our God will call" (Acts 2:38–39). I had embraced that message as a small child, as did Beatrice. This was now her first Easter with the risen Christ, in person. He is risen indeed!

James the Fox
The Unknown!

Summer 2007

Beatrice feared James the Fox. So did her sister. The fox in question was not alive. We were on a family vacation in New England, and we stopped by an antique shop to see if anything might interest us. The girls had been given money from their grandparents to spend on the trip. As we worked our way through the shop, we spotted a vintage fox fur stole with its head. When the girls spotted it, they were immediately afraid. It is also quite possible I may not have alleviated that fear and perhaps added to it by picking up the piece to scare them a bit. Perhaps a little too much fun and playfulness of a father.

However, they could not resist looking at the dead fox! All their attention was focused on it, as if the rest of the antique store was a large forest with the center of it being the fox's lair, which happened to be on a freestanding, wooden coat rack. Like timid hunters trying to be very quiet, creeping up on their game, they kept going back to the fox, trying their best to assess if this was a real threat to them. The more we lingered in the store, the braver my little hunters became. They went from steering clear of the fox with a wide berth to now touching it, then stroking its fur, and eventually holding it. Finally, they named it James. They had fallen in love with James the fox and now wanted to pool their vacation gift money to purchase it. James came home with us from New England. A once unknown terror and ferocious beast became a soft and cuddly toy that also functioned as a prop for two young pretend heiresses.

As the numbness and fog of the first year of grief wore off and the persistent and throbbing pain of a reality of life without my daughter took hold, an unrelenting terror emerged. I woke up stressed day after day with a burning compulsion to do and accomplish. Something ripe with meaning and purpose. Panic set in! There was no vision nor substance to direct my energies. The path forward was vague and nebulous, as if fog obscured what normally was a breathtaking walk through God's magnificent, landscaped paths of one's life! What if my work has no meaning to it? Am I just swimming and striving to come onshore against the ocean's tidal cycle as the water resides from the coastal shore? Am I destined for a fruitless existence? There is no hope in that life. How do you see through the fog apart from the sun burning away the cold and damp misty whispers? Panic and dread!

The unknown. In the end, I just wanted my old life back. Who wants to stare at a once beautiful and familiar garden that is now destroyed. Where do I start? I am reminded that God had once planted a garden (see Gen. 2:8–15). In His garden, He planted beautiful fruit-bearing trees, watered it by a river that flowed through His garden, and "The LORD God took the man and put him in the Garden of Eden to work it and take care of it" (Gen. 2:15). Perhaps I need to take my eyes off the garden that is no more and look to the Gardener to see where He has sown and "work it and take care of it."

Shiro

The Good Steward

August 2017

Shiro was a black-and-white spotted guinea pig. He was Beatrice's beloved pet. We found him when we were dropping off my oldest daughter for her first year in college and stopped by a local pet store for fun. There was a sign on Shiro's cage: "Free." Apparently, Shiro had been returned twice to the pet store, and no one wanted him. His only crime was that he bit his previous two owners. My guess is he had the fingers of small children poking him, and he was protecting himself the only way he knew. Bea felt pity for him and loved him at once. After a little convincing on Beatrice's part, Shiro came home with us from Massachusetts to New Jersey. We purchased a cage, food, and all the comforts a guinea pig needs. Shiro became the newest member of our household, along with our dog, rabbit, and several chickens.

While I took care of Shiro and all the other family critters in the morning before heading off to work, Beatrice did the rest. Beatrice took Shiro out of the cage and held him in a blanket and played with him. She let him run around the floor with the rabbit. Shiro had a crush on the rabbit, but it was unreciprocated. She put hats on his head and took photos. She also helped with cleaning out Shiro's cage and put out fresh water and food. Shiro was loved.

Shiro died the year that Beatrice died. It was a sad day for Bea and for all of us. As I reflect on Beatrice's life, her time with Shiro, and her death, I am reminded of a permanent fact of life I wish was not true. I am not the owner of this world. I am responsible for stewarding and appreciating what the Lord has given me and for the set time He grants. Beatrice did a fabulous job caring for one of God's smallest creatures. I am reminded of God's direction to Adam and Eve: "and rule over the fish of the sea and over the birds of the sky and over every living thing that moves on the earth" (Gen. 1:28, NASB1995). My child had "ruled" with kind, tender, and loving hands, the way her Creator had intended when He put Shiro into her hands. Well done my child.

The Great Cook
Give It a Go!

Summer 2018

Beatrice and a dear friend of hers loved to experiment with new recipes in the kitchen. Often, I went with her to the grocery store to pick out all the ingredients they needed to attempt their newest culinary creation. They measured and stirred, poured and baked. Voilà! Out came their latest cooking mystery. These two were culinary maestros.

They also found a way to use more pots, pans, bowls, utensils, and measuring cups and spoons than I ever thought possible. I didn't know we even had that many cooking things! They did most of the cleaning up, though I lent a hand from time to time.

There was one other common theme. Though they set out with the best intentions and with tasty recipes, almost everything they made was a disaster. I cannot explain what happened between the time I left them in the kitchen and the time the kitchen timer buzzed to signal completion, but catastrophe struck. The only exception to this was the lemon tart. It was the expected disaster that turned into a masterpiece—the best dessert ever produced in our house.

The exceptional quality with Beatrice was she was never deterred by the results. In fact, she was never deterred by the work involved. Once she had an idea in her head, she went to work. For her it was a matter of giving it a go and having fun along the way. The work was the work, and the results were the results. Mistakes were part of the process and added humor when things went south. Life was to be explored and enjoyed.

I purchased a car for her the year she died. She had explored much of New Jersey in it. Her favorite trip was to the New Jersey shore to see the sunrise. Getting up in the dark of morning was no hindrance compared to the joy of a sunrise over the Atlantic Ocean. She was planning a trip to the southern Atlantic Coast states for the coming spring. We also talked about me flying out to the East Coast and driving together to the West Coast, driving part of the way along Route 66. Perhaps I will do these trips for her one day. I would just need to find every quirky town and site. She would want to see that as well.

Give it a go. In some ways I am still working through being afraid of life. It has been an ongoing theme during my journey this past year. Wanting to know the outcome before starting was not a healthy way to live. During my time on the East Coast, the Lord impressed upon me to look around corners, do the work of exploration, and leave the results up to Him. That was how I was to live life. Sadly, as the first year without my daughter progressed, I had gotten more insular, more boxed into safe routines. It was opposite of what Jesus promised His disciples: "I have come that they may have life, and have it to the full" (John 10:10). I am now yearning to focus on exploration and not on safe outcomes. I have her car now, ready for new adventures. My oldest daughter drove it out to me from the East Coast. It has been traveling a fixed route for a while ever since. I think it's time to stop that and take it out on a different road! To give life a go again!

Her Life
A New Fruit

March 2002–November 2021

How do I capture Beatrice's life? I want something that will reside with me, something to make her life last within me. I was once an active participant as I watched God's mystery of her life be revealed. Reminiscent of the delight one takes hiking through God's greatest handcrafted nooks of His world, the magnificence of a human life is beyond my mind's ability to calculate and behold. It is something to be breathed and felt deep in one's soul. To be refreshed in one's spirit by the splendor and glory of His handiwork and hold her dear to my heart. How do I capture her life?

How do I share her life? Each look at Beatrice's life is unique to me, filtered through my own experiences. Though her life was shared with others, her impact on me was unique as was her impact on others. I can partially share that experience with others, but my own unique relationship with her can never be fully shared with anyone in this world. Each of us was allowed a peek as her life developed—some more than others, some only once. How do I share her life?

I know God is fully aware of the unique view I have of Beatrice's life. I could not grieve and heal apart from Him knowing fully and leading me through each area of her life that was interwoven with mine. He sees what I see and remembers every little detail I witness. I am not alone in this world then with my unique memories and thoughts. I share them with Him. The two of us have witnessed her life through the same lenses, though His lenses capture not only my unique view but everyone else's unique view of her life as well. It's a comfort to my soul knowing I am not alone in my unique view of her life.

Like grapevines from separate plants that have intertwined, never to be separated but to grow together, has Beatrice's life impacted mine. I have other close relationships that are true of this type of relationship. I think this is how God intended our closest relationships to function, branches intertwined. Her spot in the vineyard now lies vacant. Her branches still mingle with mine, but the source of life that fed those branches has been removed. The branches will never grow again nor bear such lovely fruit. How can such lovely fruit never be held again? Never to nourish the lives of others? How can these branches be without life? How can these branches no longer bear fruit? Are they destined to be forgotten, Lord?

A new fruit. What am I to do with these branches? I could allow them to decay in my soul as the years pass. I might prune them away at once from my heart. I fear for myself that either of these choices would result in a hollow existence and destroy my soul. I have one choice, and it is to allow God to graft these dead branches of her life onto my soul, giving them life and producing a new fruit neither Beatrice nor I could ever produce on our own, "a planting of the LORD for the display of his splendor" (Isa. 61:3). I am glad I chose this option. The spring buds are now emerging on these grafted branches. The fruit, I hope, will bring joy and refreshment to many hungry and thirsty souls.

Monopoly
A Legacy of Generosity

January 2011

Beatrice enjoyed Monopoly, although my oldest daughter was the tycoon when it came to the game. I lost most of the time. We modified the game a bit to make it last longer and add intrigue. Somehow, it still did not help me much. I did tend to last longer than normal but only because of both my daughters' generosity. When I was on the verge of bankruptcy, often both girls bailed me out in order to keep me in the game. My chances of victory were still zero; they were just being very sweet toward their father and loved playing.

On one occasion, when it was only Beatrice and me playing, out of the blue, she gave money to me. It was early in the game, and we both had plenty of funds, so I was not in need. The reason for her generosity? Well, in Sunday school she had been given a verse memorize: "Give, and it will be given to you. A good measure, pressed down, shaken together and running over, will be poured into your lap. For with the measure you use, it will be measured to you" (Luke 6:38). She was practicing this verse during our game.

I reminded her she was approaching my chain of hotels and would need that money if she landed on my property. It did not persuade her! Well, she soon recovered her donated funds, partly from me landing on her property with hotels. Shockingly, she avoided landing on mine during her turn around the board. Apparently, God can control the dice and instruct us from His Word at the same time.

Beatrice's generosity was not restricted to Monopoly; it was a trait that permeated her entire life. She always gave what she had to others, even at an early age. It was ingrained in her being. She always worked hard and took advantage of the many job opportunities presented to her. She then used her funds for having fun with friends and for gifts. Beatrice shared her things to a fault. Nothing was sacred when it could be enjoyed with friends and family. She never asked when in need. I always had to ask before she offered that she was in want. Such was her way of life. To give of herself!

A good measure. Beatrice focused on investing her life in others, and the work and resources then materialized for her. She had the order right. I also noticed this pattern taking shape for me during this past year in new and surprising ways. It wasn't that I was seeking a "good measure" from God; it strangely appeared. God was mysteriously caring for my needs, by unexpected means, as I was investing in the relationships He put into my life. My long-term career had always been my source of funds, until it became tenuous during this period of grief. Caring for myself and my older daughter became a concern. It became more so when I realized my healing and ability to move forward required me to leave my then current job. I had to invest my life in the people to whom God was pointing me without knowing the work opportunities nor the timing of those opportunities He would provide to supply my needs. Reckless? Perhaps! I think I just needed to put on the spectacles of generosity to see life the way God designed it to function, and the way Beatrice lived, and leave the supply to Him!

Trader Joes
A Sweet and Kind Spirit

October 2021–April 2022

Packed! The funeral house overflowed with those who knew Beatrice and our family. I prayed the Holy Spirit would show me what to say, what not to say, and what to do. With so many folks gathered, the only strength I had was from heaven. I had been praying that prayer during the week I was out on the East Coast. I was numb and had no strength to do anything apart from the strength and wisdom God granted me through my ongoing prayer.

When my dear wife (though we were no longer married at this time) arrived, we hugged each other with deep affection. An embrace of sorrow that pierced the room, I was later told. We then started to greet those who had come to honor Beatrice's legacy and support our family as we said good-bye to one of our family members. So many familiar and new faces came through. One group of new faces came up to me, four I think, and introduced themselves as my daughter's coworkers at Trader Joes. This began a procession of TJ crew members, mixed between dear friends and family. I lost count, although if someone said a dozen to eighteen TJ crew members came to the memorial, I would say that seemed correct.

One by one they gushed over my sunshine and shared stories. One was so impressed with Beatrice's work they thought she had come from another store and was shocked to realize she had only been there less than a month. Another was touched by her sweet spirit. Everything about Beatrice fit the trademark mold TJ looked for in a crew member. Indeed, her sweet and kind disposition was the rootstock in which all her wonderful traits grew and blossomed.

She was not one to procrastinate and always did abundantly more than required. I saw these traits throughout her life. She also had an unusual maturity about her, an old spirit some would say. That maturity coupled with a remarkable and extraordinary infusion of wisdom (many times both her mother and I paused and felt like God was speaking to us through her) and a deep sense of responsibility enabled her to excel at and finish whatever she started. She was smart and quick to understand. She was composed and other-centric. Her quirky personality rounded out this wonderful little Sweet Pea, a pet name my wife gave her. She also loved everything TJ had in their stores (we all did)! Thus, TJ was an ideal place for Beatrice to spend her days and energy. I just never thought it would be over after a month.

I have her nametag from her time at TJ. It is one of the articles I will keep with me until I die. During my return visit to the East Coast in 2022, I stopped by the store twice. I was greeted with open arms and heard many more stories. They had also preserved her memory by putting her nametag in both the staff room and at the front help desk. During my second stop, I met the assistant store manager, who was so glad to see me because she had not been able to come to the memorial service and wanted to pay her respects.

I was leaving the next day for Oregon, so I lingered for some time. I knew this might be the last time I visited the store, and I wanted to truly soak in that memory. I reflected on Beatrice's life as I walked the aisles and looked at all the delicious and succulent fare. Memories coming back in waves. A time of closure and healing. I also picked up a linen shopping bag, designed with pickles. I wanted something that captured my child's personality and preserved this TJ memory; she would have loved the bag. I also got a sandwich to take on the plane back to Oregon.

A kindhearted woman. Everything I needed on this visit had been accomplished, so it was time to check out. As I headed to one of the registers, the assistant store manager motioned me over to her and led me to an empty register. She wanted to pay for both items, to honor Beatrice's memory. I heard the familiar etching sound of a precious moment being engraved upon my heart. As I reflected on this day, my heart affectionately smiles at these words from Scripture: "a kindhearted woman gains honor" (Prov. 11:16). I saw this displayed by a dear and kind woman's gift to me that day, and I saw it exemplified in my child throughout her life.

A Beautiful Sunset
My Last Memory

June 2021

My two daughters and I took an Oregon road trip the summer of the year Beatrice died. As it turned out, this was the last time I saw Beatrice. We did a loop of the state and saw all our favorite spots, as well as some new ones. We gave ourselves a week and were also grateful to have Grandpa and Grandma join us for part of the adventure.

Starting in southern Oregon, we visited Crater Lake, Sunriver, and Mount Hood (for fondue of course). This was the eastern part of our trip. From Mount Hood, we then headed west, through Portland, to the rugged and beautiful northern Oregon coast and worked our way south to our most southern destination, the California redwoods. A beautiful ride back to southern Oregon along the Redwood Highway wrapped up our trip.

The highlight of the trip for me was Bandon, and perhaps for the girls as well. This quaint town along the Oregon coast was a favorite destination in the years they were growing up even though most of those times involved inclement weather and one of Oregon's specialties: rain. This day in Bandon, though, was different. It was sunny, and only a handful of clouds broke up the blue sky. This day was not dreary. The weather is always cool in Bandon, tempered by the cold Pacific Ocean, so a sunny day brings extra delight.

Bandon is known for its many monstrous rocks that line the beach, where the surf and the sand meet. We climbed upon them and, while the tide was out, explored the many caves and passageways the ocean had carved out. We took a group photo while standing in one of those caves. We also examined the diverse population of sea creatures and plants that made these rocks their home. We enjoyed every minute of our time.

The night was extra special. We ate pizza and watched as the sun descended into the west from our hotel balcony, which overlooked the ocean. The clouds turned a pale pink that deepened in shade as the sun moved to its resting spot. The sky was still, the ocean breaking so gently as photographers lined up on the beach below us to capture this whisper-blue and cotton-candy moment. I smiled at how fortunate I was to have such wonderful daughters and to share this moment with them. I liked being Beatrice's father. I am glad I can still be a father to my oldest.

My last memory. Beatrice had a deep love for the ocean. It never occurred to me this would be the last visit to the ocean with her. The last time we explored together. The last memory I had of actually being with her. The last photo taken with her! Faced with this painful truth, I found courage in these beautiful words in Scripture: "So we fix our eyes not on what is seen, but on what is unseen, since what is seen is temporary, but what is unseen is eternal" (2 Cor. 4:18). These words reminded me she is very much alive, unseen and unheard, but very much alive. I can always ask Jesus what she is doing in heaven. Worshipping, no doubt. He doesn't need to answer me. I already know she is with Him and is so joyful. Next time I'm in the cave, I will ask Beatrice and Jesus to smile for the photo. Hope others don't think I am crazy!

A Walk through the Woods
in Jacksonville
Lack of Energy

April 2022

How can I give my utmost for His highest when I can barely function? The idea of serving God drains my very being. I cannot get excited by the possibility. Even contemplating serving in the areas I loved before Beatrice's death seems overwhelming. To what purpose and end? Why do I even have to serve when I am barely functioning in life? Yet how can I not serve? What purpose do I have in life if not for His pleasure and for the benefit and refreshment of others?

Even if I were to touch someone's life in a deep and profound way, it would bring me no relief, no pleasure. All excitement has been muted because my daughter is no more. Yet since her death, I crave more meaningful and vulnerable relationships. I feel more at ease around those with deep wounds and broken lives. I think I have walked through so many dark places during my journey that I am at home around those who hurt in life. I know what it means to lose and hurt deeply, and I know the One who can mend a broken heart. I know it is slow and uneven work, and that is OK. I would rather live life along the thin line that separates sunshine and darkness, sorrow and joy. A foot in each, neither one holding sway over the other.

Maybe God is doing some new work through me. Maybe my lack of energy to serve in my old capacity is God's way of pointing me to something new He has prepared for me to do. My desires have changed since Beatrice died. So has my perspective of life, and the thought of serving God in a new capacity does sound appealing to me. I need to be content only with not rekindling something that is completed. He only gives His energy to those things He wants done. I have no energy of my own to waste on unfruitful endeavors.

It took almost a year for me to gain enough energy to even ask God more about these thoughts. A shadow started to grow, and it became clear when I recognized my motivation to get up each morning was not driven by some compelling mission in life. I got up so my mind would stop replaying everything I had lost. I now needed one purpose in life going forward. Something that would consume my energy. A fruitful and meaningful work of God.

An unexpected work. I wanted to know what to do with the rest of my life. What would be best, in service to God and others, going forward? God's words to Jeremiah reassured me: "Before I formed you in the womb I knew you, before you were born I set you apart; I appointed you as a . . ." (Jer. 1:4–5). God had something prepared for me to do. As my mind drifted over the past year, I remembered I had deferred my enrollment into a doctoral program because of Beatrice's death. From my bookshelf, I grabbed one of the books I would have read that past year. It triggered memories, thoughts, and conversations I had in the past. Over the course of that one night and quite an early start the next day, while the stars were still visible high in the sky, an unexpected work started to develop in my mind. The final version was going to take some time to fully develop, but now I would not fear the mornings with such a compelling work waiting to greet me.

A Blue Bottle, a Donut, and Muppets
My Birthday

October 2022

Bandon, Oregon—I would be spending my first birthday without Beatrice on the Oregon coast. Over the course of the first year, the Lord had been kind to me by providing plans for how to honor and remember Beatrice for each day and place that held special importance and meaning. It was now the morning of the day before my birthday, and I still did not have a plan nor any ideas about how to remember her on my day. Dread filled my heart. The fear of spending this day without some meaningful ways to grieve and remember her haunted my mind. I could face the day if He planned it for me. His plans for the first year had brought healing and closure, as well as His peace and joy, in the midst of my sorrow. This delay was palpable!

At first, I thought perhaps He was waiting for my actual birthday before telling me, but I was glad He did not wait that long. Before the day was over, He provided two special components that framed my birthday celebration. However, they were provided in a strange way, through a random stop at a local store.

I felt drawn by the Holy Spirit to stop by a familiar store. I had no idea why I was there nor what I came for, so I looked around, praying for help as to what I should grab. Then I saw it! "The Blue Bottle." A rush of memories! Beatrice was partial to Japanese things and this bottle contained a unique Japanese drink that was a favorite of ours. We only picked it up on occasions when we were out on a father and daughter adventure, and then only rarely. The perfect choice was now in my hands. A theme for my birthday began to take shape.

Pastry! She also loved pastries. Specifically, from the New Jersey bakery where I had gotten her birthday cake early that year. Well, I was in Oregon now, so I stopped by one of the best donut shops in the area and picked up one of her favorites, a pink-frosted cake donut with sprinkles. Delicious! I now had a blue bottle and a donut. Peace overflowed. The plan was coming together. Still, I knew there was something missing, so

I trusted the Lord to complete my birthday celebration and remembrance of Beatrice. And He chose to reveal the missing piece on my actual birthday.

Disney's *Muppets Most Wanted.* This was the missing piece. First seen and loved as a child, this movie was a favorite of hers. In fact, we had watched it the previous year. I laughed! I was relieved. His plan for me was now complete. I could courageously face my first birthday without her and grieve, honor, and remember her life. I now had an expectation of healing and closure as it concerned this day. Three simple things! An unexpected combination of things Beatrice loved, all filled with meaning.

With a sip from the blue bottle and a bite of a donut, I began the evening's featured movie. The movie incorporates a gulag in Siberia, a tour across Europe, a criminal mastermind named Constantine (the most dangerous criminal in the world), and all the insanity of a Muppets movie. It is filled with laughter and songs that made us smile every time we watched. I smiled as I thought of the joy and good pleasure each scene had brought to Beatrice and me. I was glad I got to relive them again. I was glad I could see the Swedish chef and his chickens again. "Classic!" This was what she said about the show. It was indeed a classic!

So, this was the way I honored her memory on my birthday—with a blue bottle, a pink donut, and a Muppets movie. The quirkiness of the evening was priceless. I am grateful to God for this plan. I am grateful for Beatrice. I finished half the drink, half the donut, and half of the movie before it got late, and it was time to go to bed. That was all I needed. My day was complete. At the same time, what a strange combination. How God can take a handful of joyful yet unrelated memories and use them to heal a broken soul is a wonderful mystery.

Two days later, I was walking on the beach of Bandon and stopped by the rocks near Face Rock, a local landmark. The tide was high, and so the caves and passages were filled with water. I started crying! I could not visit the place where I had taken my last photo of Beatrice, my oldest daughter, and me together the summer of 2021. My trip to the coast was incomplete without a trip to this rock. I needed something more. I asked the Lord what I should do and cried, "I want my child back, Lord!" It had been a while since my last deep cry, and the emotions flowed. That is when I spotted it. A long, thick, and perfectly designed stick for writing in the sand! I picked it up and started writing a note to my child in front of the rock.

Dear Bea,
> I can't wait to see you again!
> In heaven! With Jesus!
>> Love Dad

I cried more. I did not want to let her go! I wanted to hold onto her longer. The epic moments in movies of letting go are false. I don't think you let someone go in an instant. It has been gradual for me, yet her life will shape my future. I think the writing in the sand captures my ambivalence of holding on and moving into the future. The writing is a permanent reminder of her, yet when written in the sand, I know my words will be washed away by the coming high tide. It points to my desire for permanency yet crushes me with icy waves that life on this earth is not. The reality is, this beach will soon be made fresh and new, and even this mighty rock in front of me, which will endure my lifetime and many others, will one day be taken home in the beautiful waves of the Pacific Ocean. Oh, how I am grateful both Beatrice and I have a permanent home waiting for us (see John 14:1–3). She just arrived sooner than me.

The Days before Thanksgiving
The Shadows of the Approaching
One-Year Anniversary

November 2022

I am getting more anxious as Thanksgiving approaches. There is a dark dread, and I wish it would stay asleep but know it will awaken on that day. Too many emotions to process, like the waves of a fog that swiftly overtake a beautiful day. I want to be held in a deep embrace. I fear it would be only temporary comfort, and the pain from the withdrawal would be crueler than if I had never been held. I want to run away from this approaching day. More accurately, I want to run backward in time, away from this day, keeping it at bay for an eternity if possible.

Still, unless I can build a wall between today and tomorrow, never to be breached, I do not think this approaching day will ever be far from my emotions and thoughts. These days have become the worst days apart from that first day almost a year ago. The numbness has faded, and my senses are now overloaded. What a dreadful and fearful day, which cannot be stopped as it fast approaches.

Additionally, it is not only the one-year anniversary, as if all will be OK and set right when the day is complete. It is also the reality and bitter reminder that life has been altered permanently, never made whole until Jesus returns and makes all things new! So I travel along a river divided into two, wondering if they will one day rejoin. One side is swollen from winter rains, the water soil darkened, both rocks and trees carried along by its fierce strength. On the other side, the calmness of a summer day drifts along tranquil reflections and glimmering sprays. My raft ventures through both. I feel the tug of a runaway river and want to paddle hard to get out. I see, sense, and experience the calm and soothing cool of the other side. Both have my heart! Both are in contention to win the day. The tension builds with a pounding drumbeat. I am on edge as the day fast approaches.

Two components have been set in stone for some time, visiting the place I first heard the news and reading her favorite childhood book. Both seemed overwhelming to do at first. Now they are integral pieces, preciously guarded for that day and night. How the rest of the anniversary unfolds is still a mystery to me, just out of my reach and vision. Yet with the remaining components also comes courage and fortitude and the ability to fully grieve, remember, and honor my child. To allow my emotions and my memories freedom to live a lifetime in a single, sad day.

Paradise. My heart draws strength by the thoughts of heaven. It must be more spectacular than this life. Jesus said it is! (See Luke 23:42–43.) If it were not, then this approaching day, like traversing a trail that leads along the edge of the cliff of insanity, might consume me. But it will not rule my heart though the battle has drained much of my life these past days. It is my simple faith that my heavenly Father loves me and has my home in heaven prepared and decorated for my arrival that encourages me forward. Thus, I can walk amidst these dark shadows of the approaching anniversary day in confidence, fully trusting my Father to bring healing and renewal in unexpected ways on the anniversary of the darkest day of my life.

Thanksgiving
The God of All Creation

November 2022

My oldest daughter was with me that Thanksgiving morning. I was so glad to have her for the preceding few days as well. We were able to talk about our futures, each providing input into the other's plans, and this brought us both hope. It took away the anxiety of the approaching day and softened the sting of the actual day. She would fly home to New Jersey the same morning, so she could also spend Thanksgiving with her mom. We hugged at the airport and said good-bye to each other. I then texted my former wife letting her know our daughter was on her way home and shared a much more intimate and heartfelt message with her, which only a spouse could share. I ended my text with an emoji heart of love. She responded with the same. It's been hard for both of us.

Leaving the airport, I went searching for some place to grab coffee and breakfast. The cafés were dark. It was 4:30 a.m. after all. So, I headed home, went back to bed and slept for several more hours. The most important part of this day would take place later that morning, a visit to the spot I first heard the news a year ago. I planned to arrive the same time as last year and spend as much time as needed meditating on her life in conversation with God. The rest of the day would include going on a long run, preparing a side dish of asparagus, and sharing a Thanksgiving meal with my parents. The night would end with me reading Beatrice's favorite childhood bedtime story, *The Sugar Mouse Cake* by Gene Zion, before turning off the lights. A daughter celebrated, remembered, and loved.

After the additional hours of rest, I got up and leisurely got ready to face the hardest part of the day. I was lingering in my place until suddenly I felt a strong nudge by God that grew stronger, compelling me to get going. The hour and minute I first heard the news was coming fast, and I needed to be there at that exact time. I was glad I had time to make the fifteen-minute walk from my home. I needed this time to prepare myself. The place was filled with dark and painful memories, but it would also be the most meaningful and healing part of the day before closing my eyes in peace.

I arrived around 10:30, about the time I first heard the news the previous year. The bench I sat on last year was wet from the morning dew. There were also a few dried white spots from roosting birds. Fortunately, I had brought a paper towel with me and wiped off an area on the bench to sit on. My phone pinged. It was a text from my dear friend who was with me at the funeral house when I went to see Beatrice for the last time. He was praying for me!

I sat there in my thoughts and memories of Beatrice, and in prayer, for about twenty minutes. It was at this point I paused, drawn by the sounds, colors, and shifting sensations of warmth and cold, into what was going on around me. It had been going on the moment I stepped out of my house, but I was too drawn in by the moment to notice. Now with the pulse of my emotions in rest and with a crisp mind, I became an active participant in all that was taking place in God's creation as I sat on this bench.

The first notes I heard were from a symphony of birds. It was not any of the standard movements of a great symphony. It was the warmup prior to the conductor coming to the podium. A teeny bit here and there. A single chirp and sometimes together. No rhythmic timing, independent and random, yet beautiful all the same.

I was then drawn by the randomly dropping leaves, the greens of summer now painted fresh in reds, purples, crimsons, and yellows. Occasionally a green leaf was mixed in that the Painter had missed. Only the evergreens remained true to their colors, providing a wonderful complement to the temporary burst of colors of the fall season.

Still, the leaves were like puffed-up peacocks or mallards in spring trying to impress a future mate. Each leaf was broadcasting its brilliant color only to be lost within a few short days. Quick has the season of pink blossoms of youth now faded with the approaching end of a year. Their tree once held them tightly and now releases. Their lives brief, though brilliant beauty to behold. A stark reminder of the brevity of one's life in the sun and moonlight shade.

Some trees still had all their leaves while others were done, apart from a few stragglers ready to drop any day now on the gravel path and overgrown grass. The morning's translucent fog that lingered when I first arrived had now vanished. The wisp of white of my breath I could once see faded into the warmth of the full sun—no clouds today. My ears now inquisitive by the sound of a small creature as it scurried along the ground unseen, steps gentle and soft.

I felt the cool breeze hitting the back of my neck, picking up more leaves to carry to the ground. I would have shivered apart from the warm morning sun on my face and legs. A favorable tension existed between the two, neither distracting me from this morning of unexpected joy.

The multitude of birds that took the sky, each flying in its own unique way. Some glided, some glittered, some just landed in the trees. Each seemed to dance a unique dance. A waltz here, perhaps a tango there. It was a beautiful mix and array in their own way as they danced through this brilliant blue day. The blue was not uniform. Some blues were lighter, while others a bit darker, masterfully blended in the beautiful splendor of God's amazing creation.

The town had barely stirred on this quiet Thanksgiving Day except for the faint sound of cars on a back road into town, beyond the blackberry-covered fence and farmer's field next to me, where cattle roam and graze upon the grass during the summer months. The bench I was sitting on was almost dried, except for little puddles that had formed as if large tears had fallen from the sky. It was now time to head home. My time was complete. My phone chirped a second time. It was the wife of my friend who texted when I first arrived. She had picked me up at the airport when I first arrived in New Jersey a year ago. She was praying for me as well. Both her and her husband were with me in the darkness and loss a year ago. Now on the anniversary, God sent them as bookends to my time in that place of healing.

God of all creation. I had lost myself in the wonder of God's creation. It was a surprise. It was healing. He lifted my spirits up from the darkness. God had used all of His creation, including the humankind, to soothe my deep hurt and bring some joy to the day. It was a reminder that He sees and hears me. I'm glad for this beautiful day wrapped in an array of colors, leaves, grasses, trees, blue skies, and creatures of various kinds. It was something to behold. My white church sits at the end of the property. My mind drifted to the account of God's creation in the book of Genesis (chap. 1). All of His creation was good in His eyes. For six days He made everything and then rested. Beatrice is rested from her journey, as well. One day I will rest too. Though for now I will allow my senses to experience all of God's hand-iwork and thank Him for the nineteen years I had this precious handiwork to care for and love!

Letter to Beatrice
March 2023

Hi Beatrice,

I miss you, Sunshine! It has been a year and a few months since you left us. Rarely an hour goes by when you are not in the forefront of my thoughts. It is still hard to comprehend you are gone. It hurts deeply. I think it will always hurt inside though I am learning to manage better than at the beginning. Someone told me the wound from catastrophic losses leaves a deep and permanent scar. I was also told that wound needs to heal properly if you want to go on in this life with warmth, love, and purpose. This has been the challenge.

I am still scared of life though not my death anymore. The courage to take on a new adventure competes with a heart that still glances at the broken pieces, willing them back to life. It may sound like I want to be the curator at my own museum, dusty and preserved in one snapshot. I don't want that. Yet in some ways I am doing this very thing. Though I am being encouraged by our heavenly Father to embrace Him and start living with more reckless abandonment.

Happy twenty-first birthday, Beautiful! I made reservations at a nice restaurant in Jacksonville for dinner, a table for two. One for me and the other place for you. I ordered our traditional drink to start the meal and gave you a toast and wished you a happy birthday. For dinner I chose the salmon tartare, the ribeye steak (medium rare), and peach sorbet with basil. I think you would have approved of that choice. I picked up a carrot cake from Pennington Farms and ordered *Geronimo Stilton: Cat and Mouse in a Haunted House* from the local bookstore. I ate a slice of cake later that night while reading half of the book.

I finished writing *Baboons, Oceans, and a Cookie Jar*. I completed it one day before your twenty-first birthday. It felt good for it to be complete. I woke up the morning of your birthday with a deep peace, and I think I had a song on my heart as well. I read Psalm 27 that morning. I am reading through the psalms again. My time of prayer was deep and very special. Haven't had that kind of prayer in a long time. It has been hard to pray and read the Bible since you left us. The Lord has carried me all this way. I can go forward in life now that I have finished the book. The day was very emotional.

Though I shared so many of my memories of you in the book, I also left a number to reminisce with you now. I still laugh when I recall the pea-in-the-nose incident. I think you were two or three at the time. We had served peas for dinner, and for reasons only known to you, you stuck one of the peas into your nose. No one prepares a parent for such crazy circumstances; you just respond to the unpredictable. We tried our best to get it out of your nose and had no success. We called your pediatrician to ask for advice and were told to bring you in and she would dislodge the pea. So, all four of us headed to the doctor's office, a short ride for us. We checked you in and were told it would be a few minutes before you could be seen. While we waited you and your sister were playing. Suddenly, we heard a sneeze and out came the pea. Looking up to us, you asked inquisitively, "I eat that pea?"

As the author of this letter, I can choose to leave out some of the more questionable decisions I made when you were growing up. Yes, the list is extensive. No, I am not writing volume two of this book. We will focus only on a sampling and leave out the time I almost blew up the gas can, and myself in the process. It was while helping you with a school project you were filming.

I did tell the Disney story of your first ride. I may have left out a few other minor details. Yes, those things may have left permanent scars on your young mind. Yes, the Pirates of the Caribbean were much scarier than I remembered last time I was there. One of the low marks I got. Yes, The Haunted Mansion was just as bad. And yes, we should not have threatened to take you and your sister on those rides again if you misbehaved. However, I do deserve a pat on my back because I did block your eyes from seeing the monster from the movie *Alien*. I probably should not have taken you on the ride to begin with. The alien was right above your head! Big scary teeth and oozing slime. I had nightmares myself.

Also, there was no reason for our readers of this letter to be privy to our ice cream misunderstanding on that same Disney trip. Yes, I know you thought it was yours and I was eating your dessert. Perhaps I should have listened to your sister and not eaten the second of three scoops while Mom was calming you down after I ate the first scoop. When you got back, you started to scream again. The look on your mom's face made me want to cry. My bad, but it makes for a funny story. Yes! We did have a wonderful time dancing in EPCOT's Germany, and the belly dancer was a highlight for you as well when she pulled you and your sister on stage in EPCOT's Morocco. That was a fun trip.

I do miss our father-and-daughter dinners of salmon, potatoes, asparagus, and pie. I also miss not sharing life with my "baboon who lives in the tall grass." I chuckle now when I think about that memory. It truly captured your creativity, humor, fun spirit, spontaneity, and unexpectedness. You were also too precious and tender of spirit for the hardships of this world. I can't share those memories with you anymore! It is hard for me not to cry. I poured my heart into you, my precious "baboon," and it has been taken away. I must remind myself there is so much of life still to live and so much of your life that is still part of my future.

There is so much more I could capture in this letter, precious memories. However, it is time to wrap this up and keep all other memories close to my heart until we rejoin in paradise. May the glories of heaven, which are yours today, fill my heart with the hope of what is to come and strengthen my heart during the days I have been given to abandon myself to Him and to His Work.

With Deep Warmth and Love,

Your Father

Author Bio

Bryan A. Anderson spends his time between Oregon and the East Coast where he focuses his time on the spiritual revival of the banking and securities industry. He holds degrees from the University of Pennsylvania, Columbia University, Gordon Conwell Theological Seminary, and an Intermediate Certificate with Distinction from the WSET (2010, International Wine Center, New York City). Bryan has over 30 years experience in the banking and securities industry and has worked for some of the largest banking and securities firms in the world.